D1580580

Don't WASTE *Your* PAIN

Beverley Lawrence

CREATION
HOUSE PRESS
A STRANG COMPANY

DON'T WASTE YOUR PAIN by Beverley Lawrence
Published by Creation House Press
A Strang Company
600 Rinehart Road
Lake Mary, Florida 32746
www.creationhouse.com

Unless otherwise noted, all Scripture quotations are from the King James Version of the Bible.

Scripture quotations marked NIV are from the Holy Bible, New International Version. Copyright © 1973, 1978, 1984, International Bible Society. Used by permission.

Cover design by Terry Clifton

Library of Congress Control Number: 2004107759
International Standard Book Number: 1-59185-617-5

04 05 06 07 08—987654321
Printed in the United States of America

DEDICATION

I dedicate this book to every hurting and broken soul. I pray it heals your hurts and touches your soul—"Your miracle has begun."

ACKNOWLEDGMENTS

Thank you:

First and foremost the Most High God, the King of my life, Jesus.

To my husband and love, Andrew, to my strong princes, Anton and Shane, and my beautiful princess, Gabrielle. I love you guys; you have helped me turn a dream into reality. To my parents, Una and Rudy Davis, I love you both. You have given me such a strong foundation in life. To all my dear friends who have, in their own way, helped me write this book.

CONTENTS

FOREWORD

HOW REMARKABLE YOU are! You, who hold this book in your hands, who identify with its contents, and perhaps even looked for its arrival. How beloved by God is your heart, a heart which looks for the song of a new day. How precious are your soul's hands, those that reach out beyond fear, discouragement, pain and disillusionment, pushing with a silent unheralded power—power gleaned through suffering—a power in you, which will soon still vicious tongues, overcome your fears, and bring down to the ground the mountainous giants in your life.

I have written this book for *you*. It is your cry that has reached God, and though it is I who write, there is no doubt in my mind that it is He—God—who speaks. Within these pages are messages God wishes you to hear: messages of faith, hope, care, commitment, and clarity and greatest of all, His undying, unrelenting love for *you*. How I wish these messages might fly on wings with great speed to find you where you are, that they might warm your heart and soul at God's perpetual fireplace, that they might become a lifebelt to support you, an anchor to steady you, and a lighthouse to guide you past life's jagged rocks.

This book, *Don't Waste Your Pain*, belongs to *you*! It was born from my pain. Read on and listen for the gentle whispers of God's voice through its chapters, and know and be fully assured, that you are not alone!

CHAPTER 1

HONORED

W HEN YOU GET up each morning and look in the mirror, who do you see looking back at you? Who do you really see? Shall I tell you whom God sees? He sees a fighter, a pusher, a won't-stay-down, keep-coming back, in-your-face, satan, soul survivor! He sees your longing heart and hears your voice, hoarse though it is from weeping at times, and weary from hoping, but still living, still loving, still here.

God sees you, and not only does He see you, but He also honors you with such great privilege. Now why would the God of the universe honor *you*—small, weak, can hardly-make-it-through you? Because He recognizes Himself in you, you can understand that God has a longing, a longing that has spanned the reach of time, a longing that consumes His every moment, that is to find His lost image, His namesake, His heartstring, His love, and His own.

When God looks at humanity He longs to see a reflection of himself, something that even in the smallest way resembles Him. After all what father doesn't want His child, particularly His son, to look and behave like Him? God is no different. Genesis tells us that He made us, His children, in His own image and after His likeness, but that the image was lost on that fateful day in the Garden of Eden when Adam decided to disobey God.

It stands to reason that, if someone really hates your parent, be it your father or your mother, some of that hatred is going to be vented on you, particularly if you not only look but also behave like your parent. God knows the high price of suffering that we have to pay when we even remotely reflect His image. So what am I saying? What you are going through is because of your likeness to your Father God, for satan only attacks those that bear God's image. He knows He cannot take His anger, jealousy, and downright malice out on God so He takes it out on the next (thing to) God—His love, His child—you!

He will attack you to mar you, to spoil you, and to so disfigure you that you no longer resemble your Father and no longer speak like Him or act like Him. So when the darkness threatens to close in on you, you accept it and do not speak light into your circumstances as your Father God did in Genesis 1:1. So you allow it to consume you instead of doing what He did, which was move, access, evaluate, and take action. Satan does not want you to receive your Father's honor, so He will try to convince you that you bear no resemblance to Him at all.

God honors you when He sees you fall beneath your load but refuse to stay down. Why? Because that is exactly what *He* would do. He honors you when He sees that you are determined to continue in the face of adversity and criticism. Why? Because that is exactly what *He* would do. He honors you when you refuse to die even though your circumstances demand otherwise. Why? Because that is exactly how *He'd* behave if He were in the same dilemma. How often we run ourselves down for not being like Him, when in fact we resemble Him enough to warrant satan's attention.

If you really want to begin to understand the nature of God, start by reading Genesis chapter one, and there a picture of Him will emerge. As you read you will begin to realize you are very much like Him even if it is only in a few ways. He is a God who will not be intimidated, put down or run out of town by situations or circumstances; He knows what He wants and He speaks His mind; He pursues His heart's desires. He is not deterred by apparent failure; He is loving, merciful, and kind. He makes the best of a bad situation—He cares enough to try. He enjoys His own company, yet still likes to be near those who love Him. He's giving and *for*giving, He has no problem with delegating. He enjoys seeing others happy. There is so much more that I could show you, but if you have a look for yourself, I am sure you will be able to add more to my list.

His honor is about you; it is about you pushing through when you could have stayed buried under; it is about you eating humble pie when you could have had pride's caviar. It is about what you have had to speak against and what you have had to walk into (and out of). It is about what you have tasted without being wasted, what you have survived, what you cried through, crawled through, fought through, and even died through. It is about when you had to pray but did not have the words to say, so you just groaned; it is about *how* you had to pray, *where* you had to pray, *what* you had to pray, and *whom* you had to pray for. It is about how you got up when your situation said lie down. It is about you! God honors *you*!

He honors your efforts, your tears, and your determination. Despite the trials, pain, and difficulties you face, you live on! Accustomed as you may be to the tune of loneliness, rejection, resentment, and tears, you still listen for the melody of a new song. As bowed over as you may be from the weight you carry, you are not utterly destroyed. Life may be infected with bitterness at times, yet it is not poisoned. Oh, He sees you! And thus regards you as His choice vessel, His beloved, His miracle.

How often has satan injected your life with the syringe of bitterness and flooded your environment with venomous situations? Yet you live on! How often has he polluted the air about you? Yet you have not been poisoned and embittered. How often has he created mayhem and madness about you, at times leaving you feeling at the very edge of insanity's abyss? But you live on!

God, I say again, sees you. He hears and recognizes you; He honors and declares you His beloved, His miracle! But understand that the person who is loved by God is hated by satan; heaven's rose is his thorn; God's miracle is his menace, so do not expect an easy ride. Very rarely will anything you try to achieve occur without satan's intervention.

However there is good news—even at your weakest, you are still a challenge to him. The Word of God tells us that for there is hope of a tree, if it be cut down, that it will sprout again, and that the tender branch thereof will not cease. (See Job.14:7.) At this moment you may have experienced a cruel blow, but do not count yourself out; satan has not, and neither by any means has God. He has a way of creating a fountain in the most unlikely places.

Listen: satan is throwing his best shots at you, but you just will not die; you keep on getting up, again and again and again. "How can it be?" He yells at his agents. "Go back and increase the pressure. Heat the furnace—make it seven times hotter!" But one of the necessary ingredients for the maturity of a child of God is the heat of adversity. Big mistake, satan, because heat and the children of God are a lethal combination, a wonderful formula for success!

It simply infuriates satan to find that, despite all his interference, taunting, and destructive acts, you are still alive, and to make matters worse, you are still pushing. Now you may think that you are not pushing, but you are. Allow me to take a bit of time to tell you what I mean by pushing.

Pushing is getting out of bed each morning when every limb in your body is saying "lie down, curl up, and die." *Pushing* is getting yourself dressed for the day, when the day shows no sign of being dressed for you. *Pushing* is bending under the blows of life like a tree in a storm but somehow continually managing to rebound. *Pushing* is living in the worse while hoping for the better; *pushing* is looking, waiting, hoping, yearning, groaning, crying—*pushing* is what you are doing right now as you read this book!

You are pushing already not because you have learned the art of combating your problems and pain through vociferous nightly prayers, or because you have learned to recite the Bible from Genesis to Revelation; you are still in this race, this fight, on this journey, alive, because in your own way (a way that might appear pitiful, weak, and even pathetic to some), you have refused to stop pushing. Even when your mind has almost convinced your heart that it is hopeless to continue, your heart will not give up hoping, believing, and searching.

So, you see, you have been honored, and you are a miracle! Not because of what you have lost but because of what you have found—the strength, determination, courage, and tenacity to live, to *push* through your pain.

CHAPTER 2

ALIVE AND PUSHING

And Jesus went with him; and much people followed him, and thronged him. And a certain woman, which had an issue of blood twelve years, and had suffered many things of many physicians, and had spent all that she had, and was nothing bettered, but rather grew worse. When she had heard of Jesus, came in the press behind, and touched his garment. For she said, If I may touch but his clothes, I shall be whole. And straightway the fountain of her blood was dried up; and she felt in her body that she was healed of that plague.

—MARK 5:24–29

Cowering in the shadows, a weak and frail figure of a woman watched as the master passed by. Bent over and gripped with pain, broken by her persistent efforts to regain her health, she approached the wall of people that thronged around Him. Each line on her face told its own story of her anguish, of her twelve-year battle against an illness that threatened to take her life.

For in truth, it had already stolen so much from her. And yet, this merciless thief was not to be satisfied with merely ruining her entire life; it wanted more. It wanted her very breath; it wanted her dead.

With each grim diagnosis, all she ever hoped for and every aspiration were weakened. Hers was a life that bore not only physical pain, but also the pain of stigma. She was a social outcast. For her, every morning dawned with a new level of struggle, another level of anguish. How cruel this thief had been to her. The pain and suffering had reduced her to a mere shadow of her former self.

She was a woman with a problem so tragic that heaven alone held an answer. She pushed her weakened, anemic body through the crowd. Her determination was driving her on, with her thirst for life strengthening her aching limbs.

Oh, that there were some loving friends to carry her, or a miracle rod that she could stretch out over this sea of people as Moses had, so as to move them from her path!

Oh, for the strength to climb a tree, high above the throng, or for a voice to cry out to Him. But there was no rod, no friends, and no strength in her voice to call. Even if there had been, how could she call Him? She was not supposed to be out amongst these people! She was deemed unclean by the law. Yes, it seemed that even God was against her.

She had become an accursed thing, not a person any more, but an illness, a plague, a nuisance—someone people would rather forget! How could she possibly think that she could touch the Lord? She, who was unclean, messed up, dirty! Indeed, everything she touched was regarded as unclean. Nevertheless, she silently pushed.

Do not think for one moment that hers was a lesser task than that of Moses. Should we assume that Moses demonstrated more belief in God's ability to get the job done than this woman? No! As the apparent impossibility of parting the waters of the Red Sea faced Moses, so the impossibility of a woman breaking through this potentially hostile crowd loomed before her. As did Moses, she exercised powerful, God-moving faith.

This woman, afraid, alone, a prisoner in her own body, dared to push through her pain. Her very existence was incredible, a miracle in itself. How was it possible that she was still alive? Surely she should have passed away long ago. Yet she defied every prognosis made by the doctors, each flippant word from her peers and the scorn of society. Like the olive yielding its oil under intense pressure, so this woman's faith yielded itself in her push, her struggle to touch the Master.

It had been twelve years since her life substance had begun draining away. She was hemorrhaging, literally bleeding to death. The memory of a life before bleeding faded with each passing year. Life before then seemed like a dream, perhaps too painful to recall.

I am sure this woman had friends, family, money, love, esteem in the community—yet how quickly everything had changed!

As the fetid odor of her life substance clung to her dying body, she pushed herself on. She had given everything to get her life back; she had spent all and was all spent; she was dying to live again, dying to laugh again, dying just to be made whole.

A SPENT-ALL PUSH

All of this woman's efforts in attempting to help herself had left her in the position of having spent all. But I have come to understand God's deep love for spent-all people. These are people who feel that they have nothing left to give—not love, not tears, not laughter, nothing. He knows exactly how it feels to have spent all.

After the fall of Adam, God tried everything throughout the ages to bring His lost sons back to Him. It appeared that no amount of sacrifice could do it, that nothing could permanently bridge the gap between God and man and heal man's gaping wounds. Yet God would stop at nothing; if it meant giving up His only Son, then He would, and He ultimately did.

One day, as Jesus sat near the treasury, He watched, as all the rich men cast in their gifts. However, He was not moved by them. What moved Him was a certain poor widow casting in her two mites. So touched was He by her offering that He pointed her out to His disciples saying, "Verily I say unto you, That this poor widow hath cast more in, than all they which have cast into the treasury: For all they did cast in of their abundance; but of her want did cast in all that she had, even all her living" (Mark 12:43–44).

God spent all in the person of Jesus Christ. He was everything that heaven had to offer. God knows what you are going through when you feel as if you have nothing left. So press on! Keep pushing! Even Almighty God had to!

Every time we try to push beyond our affliction, there will always be countless reasons not to. The very thought of, "What will happen if I do?" can stand as a giant before us, overshadowing the more vital question of, "What will happen if I don't?"

The woman knew the penalty for being caught in the crowd. She knew she could be stoned to death, I believe she fully weighed up the consequences and still decided to push. She must have thought it through before she left her house that day. Her need to be healed far outweighed her fear of being caught and stoned.

How much do you want what you need? Understand that the depth of our thirst determines how much we drink, and this woman was parched. So yes, I can imagine that as she got dressed that morning she counted the cost: now, what have I got to lose?

- My life? I am already dying.

- My reputation? *What* reputation?

- My money? I have spent it all on those so-called doctors!

- My friends? They have long gone!

Now, I dare to say that this woman at her weakest was in the strongest position she had ever been in. She was stronger now than she could ever have imagined. We cannot begin to fathom what God can do through our weakness. It makes no possible sense that one deemed as contemptible and sinful could experience God's incredible metamorphic power, a transformation that is worthy of Creation's awe-inspired sigh!

Listen, this woman's moment of glory did not come through her strength; it came through her weakness, through her pain. Suddenly, all her pushing paid off; for there in front of her, within her reach, was Jesus! With her heart racing and her body crouched, she timidly stretched a trembling, but determined, hand out to touch His clothing. The Bible

11

tells us that she received her healing immediately!

What unfeigned bravery this woman displayed in her quest for life! What unstoppable passion! There must have been times when she did not feel she could go on, yet on she went, on and on until she forced her dream into reality. Her impossible dream, the long awaited dream of a cure finally came true.

When Jesus asked, "Who touched Me?" the crowds parted to find her, cured but cowering, but Jesus merely added the final touch to her healing by declaring, "Thy faith hath made thee whole." Her cowering days were over; she was healed, truly healed, and she would never have to cower again!

When you are willing to take a chance on life, to push beyond fears and the normal mode of your existence to achieve your dream, your cowering days will come to an end, just as this woman's did.

Jesus recognized that it had taken nothing less than persistent, determined, crowd-moving faith for her to reach Him. He looked at the size of the crowd and the potential hostility she had subjected herself to, and acknowledged her incredible courage. He recognized that no less than this kind of courage would enable Him to carry out His daunting task. For just as she had pushed past the force of the crowd to touch Him, Jesus knew that the time was fast approaching when *He* would have to push past the veil of His flesh to touch the holiest of holies for the healing of all mankind.

There is a power that comes through our weakness, and this paradoxical power has, over the centuries, mystified logic, overthrown tyranny, conquered the grave, slain giants, destroyed dark realms, and silenced the accusing tongue of the devil. My friend, do not write yourself off because you feel you have nothing left to offer God but your tears, or what you consider to be your failings. God has a bright purpose for you!

Consider this woman, how long she suffered—twelve years! But still she conquered at a time of life when no one would have expected her to. She reached out through her weakness and touched a miracle, becoming one herself. God's glorious word to us is that the weak declare themselves to be strong. Is this power coming through strength? No, it is power coming through weakness!

ALL-SPENT SONS

You could not get more all-spent than Jesus; yet nonetheless, He pushed through His weakness, agonizing in the garden with the taste of the bitter cup of death on His lips. He fell on His face and cried, "O my Father, if it be possible, let this cup pass from me: nevertheless not as I will, but as thou wilt" (Matt. 26:39).

Never before had the shadow of the cross appeared so close to Him as in the Garden of Gethsemane. Here it towered over Him. Jesus in His humanity became afraid. The task ahead of Him appeared painfully impossible. He needed His Father's assurance. He cried the same prayer three times, and each time He was left to find His Father's desired answer, "Nevertheless not as I will" (Matt. 26:39).

We all have to reach a place in our walk with God, when His resolve, His mind, and His will become totally ours, not merely in our pleasant mountain-top moments, but in our bitter valley of shadow times, as well.

Jesus was in this valley, except that this time, unlike in David's psalm, this was not the shadow, but the caster of the shadow. Jesus was staring death right in the face. Some of us might think that being Jesus made it easier to perform the will of His Father and bear the pain and anguish. On the contrary, His name and His position made it no less difficult. Jesus was hurting, just as any of us would be, if faced with the task He had chosen to carry out.

Letting go of what we want for what God requires of us is not always easy. Finding that level of selflessness is a journey not to be scoffed at. Yet the rewards for those who would aspire to selflessness in God far exceed any pain they have to endure to reach it.

Now, for the first time in His life, Jesus called His Father and there was no response. The experience was one He had never encountered before. He had always had His Father's immediate reply. They were constantly communicating with each other; but this time He called, and there was no open heaven, no descending dove to light upon His head, no familiar thundering voice for all to hear, no angels to minister to him. He was alone.

As Jesus hung on the cross, with His voice breaking under the intense pain, He cried, "My God, my God, why hast thou forsaken me?" (Matt. 27:46). It was a cry that bore no resemblance to the one when He had commanded Lazarus to come forth, or the one when He had forced the demons of sickness from their victims. No, this frail, broken figure bore no likeness to the Mighty One who stood on a ship in the midst of a storm, who spoke to the wind and the waves, commanding their immediate obedience. Jesus hung there alone, a heart-rending picture of an all-spent son.

He had spent three and a half years of His life with His disciples, sharing His heart with them as they went everywhere and did everything together. Yet when He needed them the most, they fled for their lives in fear. All the people who waved palms in the streets of Jerusalem and sang "hosanna" as He rode in on an ass were now singing another song, one which tune contained the words "crucify Him." Most of those He had healed, transformed, and given hope to were gone. He was clubbed, spat upon, ridiculed, and rejected.

Stretched out naked like the mighty oak tree in the winter, He hung there. The beauty of His leaves and His covering were gone. His branches were now exposed to the devil, with cold, windy lashes and the devil's eerie howls and taunts of laughter. "Thou that destroyest the temple, and buildest it in three days, save thyself. If thou be the Son of God, come down from the cross!" (Matt. 27:40). Jesus was left alone to bear the pain of satan's mocking.

Greeted no more by the mellow rays of the sun, nor the sky's warm breeze, but rather by the chilly sneers of the wintry gale, God, the sun of His life, was gone, hidden away behind the clouds. He was bleeding and dying, exposed now to the piercing cruel claws of the ravens and vultures that came callously looking for somewhere to perch, for somewhere to sharpen their beaks. The former splendor of His blossoms seemed long gone.

Gone too were the birds that once nested here. Gone was the beauty of their songs. His devotees dwindled now to a small, pitiful handful. Greater in number were those who came to mock His fate than those who came to mourn His demise. This was the season that this green tree most dreaded—winter.

Perhaps if Isaiah, the eagle-eyed prophet, who had prophesied hundreds of years before the birth of this all-spent Son

(Isa. 9:6), had been permitted to look a bit further down the corridors of time into heaven's courtrooms, I imagine he would have heard the lament of the angels as they listened to their sovereign cry out under the lashes of the whips and groan under the load of His cross.

Or possibly he would have heard the mighty voice of the Archangel Michael echoing along heaven's hallways, prayerfully entreating God to give him the authorization to intervene. Perhaps he would have witnessed an angel swiftly nudging forward Simon of Cyrene to help Jesus with the cross. Possibly He would have written that the thunder and earthquake that followed Jesus' death was a result of the angels sorrowfully folding their wings together and bowing their heads to the ground on that cruel day, when the kingdom of heaven stood silent and the kingdom of hell rejoiced.

But we see Jesus unashamed of His naked pain, standing even taller in a wondrous display of power, the kind of power that is at its best in humble, obedient submission to the will of God. Not a "what I will" power but a "thy will be done" power. A power that is often not recognized, but rather one that is laughed and jeered at but given to those who yield themselves to God's will.

Jesus, His strength all spent, His body weak from sleep deprivation, hungry, thirsty and bleeding, pushed beyond the veil of His flesh and its desires. Dressed in the clothes of our unrighteousness, under the painful weight of our curse, accomplished the impossible. He was accustomed to doing the impossible, but this time it was not through His strength or His power; it was through His weakness.

The greatest achievement that you will ever accomplish in your life will not come through your strength but through your weakness. It will come at a time when you think you just cannot take any more, at a time when you are just about down and out. When it happens from that standpoint you will always ascribe your glory to its rightful owner. You will never again look down on the weak or insignificant things of this life. You will know the true roots of real power.

Which man will demonstrate the sort of compassion that will change lives? Which one, I ask you: the man who has known weakness? Or the man who has only known strength?

From an all-spent stance, Jesus pushed past the taunts, heckles, and accusations of the devil to produce abundant life! It is this that God desires of you, my friend, that you push from your all-spent stance, that you push through your weakness. Regardless of whether you are able to hear or feel Him, and even when it appears that heaven's doors are wide open to everyone else but you, PUSH!

Yes there will be times when you feel so dejected and despondent, days when you feel unable to push. But you have to resist responding to what you feel or see, and go by what you hear! Why? Because Scripture tells us, "So then faith cometh by hearing, and hearing by the word of God" (Rom.10:17). So hear and receive this Word of God that I give to you, "You can push through your pain. You can and you will! For God wills it so!"

The Bible tells us that after a long period of drought Elijah heard the rain before He saw it. "But that's impossible," I hear you say, "How can we hear rain before we see it falling?" My reply is, "By faith's ears!" With the ears of faith you can hear your miracle before it arrives! You can see it before it materializes and celebrate in confident anticipation. (See1 Kings 18:44.)

17

Understand this: in the kingdom of God things are not always as they appear. Just because you cannot see your deliverance doesn't mean that it is not happening. How often have you stood waiting for a train and heard it long before it came into sight? Your deliverance is no different! You will hear it sometimes through the words of a friend, a preacher, a prophet, or a perfect stranger even long before you see it. Just because you cannot see something does not mean it is not there. So stand your ground, no matter how spent you feel. Listen for the sound of victory, blessing, deliverance, and healing! Hear it and rejoice, for it is on its way, and it is being heralded for you.

Also accept that your condition is not your conclusion. God would not bid you to push through your weakness if He knew you were unable to; He knows you can beat what is trying to beat you. You can touch God from an all-spent stance. It is certain that you are bound to be healed, bound to be set free, bound to win! It is impossible to lose even when everything says you *have* lost. Jesus made sure of that when He got up from the grave's grip after three days and three nights. Nothing can hold you down, because He got up! Nothing can keep you back, because He pushed forward! Nothing can keep you bound, because He declares you to be free! Whom Jesus Christ set free is free indeed! (See John 8:36.)

CHAPTER 3

DON'T WASTE YOUR PAIN

I NOTICED AN ELDERLY, somewhat large, African Caribbean midwife, peering over the nurses gathered at my bed she was staring hard at me. Suddenly, without a word to anyone, she lunged forward, took hold of my hand, and squeezed it tightly. Her grip demanded my immediate attention, which up till then, no one had been able to gain. Her voice was firm. "Beverley," she said, moving closer to me, her eyes widening, "You're wasting the pain." Of all the things I expected her to say this was certainly not it.

I was expecting words to the effect of, "It's going to be alright," or "You're doing good, honey," or even "Yes, I know it's hard, but it will all be over soon." All or any of these would have worked for me, but certainly not, "You're wasting the pain!"

Looking deep into my eyes as though reading my thoughts of objection, she defiantly said again, "Yes, you are! You're wasting the pain."

Who was this woman anyway? It was just typical that of all the labor rooms in the vast hospital she had to choose mine! She was the last person I needed, or indeed wanted, at my bedside. I wanted a pain reliever, not a pain believer!

As the pain intensified with each contraction, a million thoughts raced through my mind. How could this woman tell me that I was wasting pain, as though it were some precious commodity? I had heard of wasting money, wasting time, wasting energy, but not wasting pain! I mean, come on, pain is just pain! Right? How can it be wasted? It is just what it is, pain.

My eyes quickly scanned her uniform. Was she wearing a midwifery badge? Was she for real? But to my horror it was there; she *was* for real, and I was in real trouble, or so I thought.

One by one the other nurses began to leave my room. "Why were they leaving me with her?" my brain cells yelled. Hadn't they heard what she had said to me about wasting pain? Why were they leaving me in the hands of a sadist? Just as I was about to call for them to stay, another contraction hit me, throwing me forward, straight into this woman's arms. But by this point I did not much care what she was saying or doing, I just wanted the pain to stop. If you did not know this already, pain has a strange way of humbling you.

Brushing my hair back, then moving her hand to my stomach, she said, "Now when you feel the pain, push, push through the pain. Don't waste it! It's there for a reason; so don't fight against it, but use it to push."

Don't Waste Your Pain

As I heeded her advice, my pain became secondary to delivering my child, and changing my focus, I channeled all my strength into bringing my baby into sight. It was amazing: just as she had said the pain did in fact help me to push; it came as a sort of indicator of when to push. As soon as I changed my perception of it, it did not hurt any less. But it in some strange way, humbled, prepared, and focused me.

No one likes pain; no one relishes the thought of being sick or going through a painful experiences. Yet I have come to understand that all new life is birthed through a level of pain. Often we see great men and women in this world and wonder how they are that way; how they got to where they are. The answer is by preserving through and triumphing over their trials.

Now do not get me wrong: I am not some sort of sadist who relishes the thought of painful experiences! I have simply come to understand that great power comes through great struggle.

A baby's birth means his mother's pain, her struggle. She has a choice. She can fight the pain, but why? She would be obstructing the vehicle by which her desire is being ushered in. And though her struggle may become increasingly intense, she must push through it if she is to hold her baby at the end of the day.

Where are you right now? In a place of pain or struggle? Understand that your pain has a purpose; do not waste it. Yes, it hurts when the one you love rejects you, or when your world seems to be falling apart and there appears to be no one to turn to, or when you have been used and abused, but there is a reason for your pain; again I say, "Don't waste it, push!"

Crying over the things that have passed is wasting it. Weeping about the unfairness is wasting it. Lying back and giving up is wasting it. Shutting down and closing everyone out is wasting it. Allowing your pain to make you become unforgiving and bitter is wasting it. Do not allow yourself to waste it!

Do you know that it was God who was the first to experience the horror and utter pain of loss? When satan fell from heaven, he took two-thirds of the angels with him. God was the first to experience the pain, grief, anguish, and the utter void of losing a child—Jesus on the cross. God was rejected as a parent before anyone else, when Adam and Eve chose to listen to satan over Him.

You have been through too much; you have cried for too long to allow purely your pain to be your reward. Do not stop there; do not die at the threshold of your blessing, but push on and take hold and embrace your real reward. Too many of us, like Rachel, the patriarch Jacob's wife, die before we see our reward. We die on the threshold of our new life.

Do not die now, but live on! Do not let go and get swept away in a sea of self-pity, bitterness, and sorrow. Live! Your pain has not come to destroy you, but rather to usher you into a new life, with new possibilities! To stop at your pain is surely to lose the powerful results it is producing. To die now is not to embrace the wonderful things that are before you! Stop crying over the things you think you have lost, and look to the things that God wants you to gain. This God, whom I have come to know, has an incredible way of giving back the things that you have lost, fourfold!

Life holds many disappointments, but at the same time it holds many more opportunities! What are you focusing on, the disappointments or the opportunities? Know this, that by overly taking notice of your disappointments you lessen the likelihood of seeing your God-given opportunities. Dwelling on your disappointments will only serve to keep you disappointed, resentful, and sad. But if you can find the strength to look away, for even one moment, you will find in that moment more than your disappointment has ever showed you. You will see a whole new realm of opportunities that you never realized were there. Within each of us is newness, brilliance, and much, much more! But without the courage to be humble, selflessness to be obedient to the will of God, and vision to stay focused, that newness will never be realized!

To return briefly to my labor-room experience: I was pregnant with life, a new wondrous gift which was once hidden, once small and unseen, had now grown to full term and stretching out inside of me, ready and waiting to be released, and what was I doing? Screaming, crying, and focusing on the struggle, drowning in my pain, rather than ushering in my gift. It is all too easy, if we are not careful, to allow purely our pain to be our portion. My misdirected focus was making my pain appear worse, and my struggle unbearable, like a magnifying glass amplifying my state out of all reasonable proportion.

In a world where more and more women are opting out of childbirth for fear of losing their figures or for dread of labor pain, the temptation to look for quick fixes and easy routes in our walk with God appears increasingly appealing. However, we must not allow ourselves to accept anything less than what God asks for, and what He asks for is faithful focus, for no less than that yields God's desired fruit.

Like the mother pushing to bear her child against the

forces of pain, or the salmon swimming upstream against the river's torrential current to lay her eggs, or the pilot flying the airplane high into the sky against the forces of gravity to reach his desired altitude, so we have to focus and push against the distractions, struggles, pain, and adversities that come against us in our daily lives, in order to accomplish God's purpose for our lives!

God knows that it is not easy to find focus when trouble, worry, and struggles are the loudest voices in your life, or to have the courage to push when all previous attempts have fallen well below expectations, or to have clear vision when your skies are dark with thunder clouds. Yet focus you must!

He recognizes how difficult it is to find the determination to believe that your life can be reborn as wonderful, when it appears to be a graveyard of aborted hopes and miscarried dreams. But you have to believe that you will find a wonder yet to be born, a joy yet to be expressed, and a beauty yet to be displayed.

God's Word declares that all things work together for good for them that love God, for those who are called according to His purpose (Rom. 8:28, author's paraphrase). Everything that has caused you pain, all the struggles and the disappointment are catalysts for good. Isn't that amazing? How can experiences that feel so bad, and can appear so incredibly insane, work to bring about anything good? The answer is that God is doing the working; you are not alone.

CHANGE YOUR FOCUS

The need for godly single-mindedness in our walk in this time of continual satanic attack is essential. It is difficult—in fact, almost impossible—to envisage us attaining the prize of our high calling in Christ Jesus without godly focus.

There is an old adage that says, "We are what we eat." Allow me to give an example of this adage. Show me an extremely overweight person and I will show you too much sugar, fats, carbohydrates, and not enough exercise. Now that might sound hard and uncaring, but it is simply the truth. That same adage changed slightly can be used to bring across my point about godly focus. Show me your focus and I will show you its results.

It is essential that we realize that our lives illustrate our focus. Whatever we allow our focus to be is what we will ultimately produce. For example, if all you think about every day is how much you dislike a certain person, be sure that the only thing you are going to produce is bitterness, hatred, and malice. Here is another illustration: let's say you had an argument with your husband and, no matter how many times he tells you that he is sorry, all you can think of is how much he hurt you. Your product at the end of the day will be a hardened heart, bitterness, unforgiveness, mistrust, and possibly even a broken marriage. Do you see?

It is crucial that we watch our focus in all areas of our lives, as it will sooner or later determine our harvest. The Bible puts it this way, "Set your affection on things above, not on things on the earth" (Col. 3:2). In other words, if you want to gain those heavenly things, fix your sights on God. Very soon you will become godly. In another

Scripture Jesus tells His disciples: "Seek ye first the kingdom of God, and all his righteousness" (Matt. 6:33), again demonstrating the same thing—focus.

Often we consider failure as something to be embarrassed about or ashamed of, when we really should be seeing our failures as lessons—learning processes for future successes! Think about it: how did you learn any of what you currently know? Wasn't it through a series of failures? Perhaps not all, but at least some? Failure is as much a part of success as passing or winning. When we begin to understand this we will not be afraid or deterred by our failures.

The greatest inventions of life all came about through a series of failures. George Stephenson did not get his invention of the steam locomotive right the first, second, or the third time. Neither did Alexander Flemming in his discovery of penicillin. I could list countless names of men and women who pushed beyond failure to produce great wonders, some of which have changed the very course of history. So never let go of your dream, no matter how many times it has failed to materialize. Keep pushing!

Hold a camera in your hands and look through its lens without adjusting it for focus, and all you will see is a blur regardless of how beautiful a scene the camera is aimed at. Now take that same camera, point it at the same scene but this time adjust its focus, and the results are amazing— sharp crystal clarity, beauty, colour, and precision all this from a simple adjustment of focus. What I am attempting to show is that regardless of the beauty of God's plans for you, you have the power of focus, so make sure you use it wisely, to see the things of God and not the blurred confusion of satan. Without focus God's vision will simply not be seen as anything but a confusing blur.

What a difference focus makes, not only in our outlook but also in our attitudes and actions. Two people stand at a window looking out over a meadow steeped in the colours of summer. One looks through a focused lens and the other through an unfocused one. Who leaves the room touched and inspired? The one with the focused lens or the one without?

It is interesting to note the many men and women who have faced adversity and remained *overcomers*. How did they do it? By persistent worrying and fretting or by focusing? Focus: it is how the man, Nelson Mandela, overcame the injustice of his cruel thirty-year prison sentence, to rise to become president of the very country that had imprisoned him. And how the man, Franklin D. Roosevelt, came to stand as one of America's greatest presidents, leading his country through a time of great depression and through the Second World War, although he was painfully afflicted by polio.

Note that I deliberately used the word *man*, before making reference to each of these people. Why? Because many of us have a way of putting such "overcomers" on a pedestal of super humanness, implying that their achievements are beyond those of us everyday normal folk. But the fact is that these people were not and are not super humans. They were and are everyday folk, just like you and me. They had no special powers or secret potions—far from it! They had their bad days of pain, failure, and discouragement, just as you and I do. But they added to those days *focus*, not just any old focus, but a faith—an adjusted focus.

Certainly it would have been easy for any of them to remain in a blurred, confused state of discouragement when disappointment and tragedy came knocking. But with faith adjusting their focus, they were able to see a picture that far surpassed the ugliness of the present; a picture so wonderful and a future so bright that it propelled them forward, giving them an almost supernatural determination and a resilience that made men and women stop and listen, respect and follow. My friend, if you would just add to your life a *faith-adjusted focus*, you would be astounded at what you would see!

There is a characteristic, I have found, that runs through the lives of every conqueror and every overcomer, a characteristic that I know lies in you too. It is a refusal to be beaten, to give in, to let go; a stickability and an adaptability that is amazing. I call them "whatever-the-weather" folk, because if their sunny days turn to rainy stormy days, they do not spend much time resenting the weather; they simply change their attire to suit the conditions. Very rarely can they be found weeping miserably in the rain! No, these "whatever-the-weather" folk use all of what they experience to become all of what they can be.

So why will you overcome all that you are going through to achieve the unbelievable despite your pain? The answer is within you and has always been within you. You have the power to change—or indeed *not* change—your focus. It is all up to you!

CHAPTER 4

GET AN ATTITUDE

THERE IS A type of push that cannot really be called impolite, although under normal circumstances it could quite easily be considered so. This push is in no way normal, ordinary, or everyday. It is a push recognized by its desperation and longing. It cannot be silenced, appeased, or patronized by refinements, protocols or the status quo. Its fulfillment can only be found in its complete release. It is the push of the all-spent, of the desperate, of those who have nothing left to lose.

Casting my mind back to my labor-room experience tells me in no uncertain terms that it is possible to reach a time in our lives when the sign on the door reads, "Refinements are of no use here." This is a time when there can be no room given to any form of sophistication which will in any way hinder your progress.

My labor-room experience wasn't the place for "if you please," "excuse-me" glamorous hairstyles and make-up, or even timely, well rehearsed ante-natal class panting. Real life doesn't always go by the book. The reality and severity of my pain determined my decorum, and, believe me, my pain must have registered on the Richter scale. So I will leave you to imagine my decorum! I had at that moment to find the attitude of the pusher, and what was that attitude? Simply, to push!

The Bible tells of a woman whose husband was one of the prophets in Elijah's school of prophets; he died suddenly, leaving his wife and sons in serious debt. Unlike today, the men in biblical times were very much the providers or breadwinners in their homes. Consequently, this man's death had devastating results for his family, the most urgent and weightiest of which, according to the biblical account, was financial. (See 2 Kings 4.)

At his death, this woman, for whom the Bible gives no name, and her sons were left to the mercy of their creditors, who were known for their mercilessness. Now in the light of her situation and with the weight of her financial dilemma, it would have been understandable if she had decided to let go and wait to be washed away in a flood of anguish, grief, and sorrow. But she did neither of these things; instead, she directed her focus and energy on pushing for *the* solution. Note I have used the phrase "*the* solution" as opposed to "*a* solution," for there is a stark difference between the two.

"'A solution" speaks of one of many solutions, which do not necessarily give the required answer, while "the solution" speaks of the unequivocal answer. One can always find a solution. But that does not mean it is the right one. It is as haphazard, in terms of accuracy, as picking a name out of a hat. However, when one finds *the* solution, the same hat is used; but in this case, there are no other names in the hat, just one. That is to say, "*the* solution."

So this nameless but determined woman went straight to Elijah the prophet and demanded that he do something to help her. In essence, she was refusing to be a victim. She displayed the mindset that God wishes for all of us, the mindset that says no matter what we go through, or what we have to face, we should never consider ourselves victims, or even survivors, but victors!

One can almost immediately gauge her self-image, just by observing this woman's actions and attitude. She demonstrated the attitude of a pusher. It was the image of a conqueror. It shouted, "I'm not accepting this; yes, my husband is dead, but *I'm* not! I refuse to go down without a fight!" Remember what I said earlier about Nelson Mandela and President Roosevelt? Can you see the similarities in this woman?

Listen, life will not always deal us good cards. Indeed, sometimes the hand we are dealt appears far from fair, but what are we going to do? Sit and weep about it, or push beyond it? So what are your actions shouting out about *you*, I wonder? Take a moment to think about how you are handling your problems. Is there anything you are not doing that you could be doing? Or is there anything that you *are* doing that you shouldn't be? Can you learn from this woman? I know I did!

The woman commanded and assembled her thoughts, strength, faith, and belief. She pressed the eject button on feelings of weakness, doubt, and fear. She pushed for *the* solution to her calamity. Refusing to be crushed by the crisis, she didn't waste her pain, but used it as a battering ram to push for a miracle! Like a mother-to-be pushing through her contractions to bear her child, this woman pushed for more, for what was rightly hers, for a miracle! And, do you know something? She got it, and so will you! So catch her attitude!

Destiny's Contractions

Life has its contractions; God inseminates each life with purpose—a purpose placed deep within the womb of our souls, there to await life's contractions (our difficult experiences) to bring us to our destinies.

Before Mary, the mother of the Savior of the world, was birthed into her divine purpose, she suffered the shame of pregnancy outside of wedlock and the fear of public exposure. Before David could attain his destined purpose he had to endure the resentful mindset of his brother and a fight with a giant, suffer the loss of a faithful friend, and endure the hatred of a king. Before Jesus could declare, "The Spirit of the Lord is upon me," He had to go through the isolation and hunger of the wilderness and the intense onslaught of temptation from the devil. To every man or woman who would walk in the divine purpose come the contractions of destiny. Who can tell how long yours will last? But when it is all over—oh, the glory!

Broken Is Not Useless

A horse once ran every major race for its owner, and although he had won many of them, it appeared that he was losing form, as he suddenly began to lose race after race. His owner had become famous through him and had made vast amounts of money from his races, yet he was fast beginning to tire and grow intolerant of his horse's loss of form.

One day whilst galloping towards the finishing line in a high-stakes race, the horse tripped and fell. The crowd gasped. While the jockey emerged uninjured, the same could not be said of the horse, whose injuries were critical. "Put Him down," his owner instructed the vet, "he's of no use to me injured." As the vet prepared to administer the lethal needle, a voice from the beyond the crowd called, "*I'll* buy the horse." "Like I said," his owner replied, "He's of no use to me injured; to be frank, he's good for nothing." "No matter," the lone voice replied. "I still want Him."

Isn't it amazing that God, like that lone voice in the crowd, has carried out that same act of kindness for us— that He watches our crowded, pressurized lives from a distance, blocked out by the crowds we surround ourselves with. And we like the horse, silently injured, tired and disheartened, continue to race, running towards nowhere, ever racing, yet never winning, never truly achieving anything but the fleeting praises and acclaim of a fickle favor.

God watches us, knowing that soon we will fall broken, unable to continue. He watches not to gloat, but to be at hand for our inevitable demise and satan's cruel demand. It is God who shows us through our injured lives that broken in no way equals useless. He has no reservations about investing His time in nurturing and aiding us to be all that we can be, accomplishing this by literally putting perfection—Himself—inside of imperfection, us!

He, like the pitch that Noah used to seal the Ark, fills every crack, hole, and crevice in our lives, making us storm resistant and watertight. He brings healing and beauty to all that is ugly, bitter, and damaged in us.

It is indeed marvelous that, even though at times we fall before him broken, cast down and sick or struggling with habits and proclivities, with pains and regrets in our crowded lives, God still declares us to be people of purpose—a purpose that is godly and divine. It is a purpose that no one but you can wipe away, erase, reverse, destroy or kill. It is a purpose placed inside us, with the confidence that we are of worth, and that however we or others see ourselves, we are by no means useless, not while we are in *His* hands. In the capable hands of God nothing is useless, nothing.

CHAPTER 5

MY TURN, FOR A CHANGE

THE BIBLE INTRODUCES us to a man in the fifth chapter of John's Gospel, who had endured a certain sickness for thirty-eight years of his life, a sickness that had deprived him of the use of his legs.

Now thirty-eight years is a long time even for one who is able-bodied, but to be ill for this length of time must have felt like an eternity. To wake each morning with the hope of healing pounding in his chest, only to have that hope repeatedly dashed, must have been heartbreaking. To witness others receiving what he so earnestly desired for himself was surely agonizing! To feel that once-excited hope drain away at the end of each unanswered day is beyond comprehension. Yet the Bible's account of this man is that he was living exactly as I have described.

He lay among the multitude of impotent folk, all gathered

in the five porches of Bethesda waiting for their only chance of a normal life. It was known that at a certain season, an angel would descend into the pool there, to stir up its water with healing virtue. It was a miraculous occurrence, which demanded a strange, almost unfair criterion from those who would be healed. The first person to manage to get into the pool after the angel had troubled the water was immediately healed of his or her sickness, but anyone who stepped in after that was denied.

The profound pain and frustration, shame, rejection, and perhaps even anger this man must have felt, is unimaginable—not only because of his crippling infirmity, but from watching others receive what he so wanted and indeed deserved. It was not that he had not tried; he *had*. But each time, he was beaten to the pool by someone more able-bodied than he.

What made him any less deserving of the blessing and healing than all those who had received theirs ahead of him? Surely he was no more sinful than they, and his need was just as great as anyone else's! But perhaps there *was* a reason why he, though in the right place at the right time, kept missing his turn for a miracle—a wrong attitude that affected his focus!

You see, he felt he could only receive his healing if he was helped by others into the pool. But the problem was that there never seemed to be anyone there when he needed them the most! Have you ever felt like that? Have you ever thought your help would come from your friends, your neighbors, or your family, only to discover that when you needed them most, they were not there for you? Well this man had not only been there, he had lived his life there for thirty-eight years. But Jesus was about to change all this;

My Turn, for a Change

He was about to change his address from, "I can do it if my friends help me" to "I can do all things through Christ."

It had been thirty-eight years of putting his trust in others and waiting for their help. It had been a lifetime of begging, expecting, and waiting, depending on some-one—*anyone*—to help him out of his misery and into his healing.

How he managed to look beyond the misery of his squalid existence is a miracle in itself, as he continually witnessed everyone else's healing, but never his own. Perhaps it was the man's tenacious, almost pathetic determination, that drew Jesus' attention to him, that led Jesus to reveal that the strength he needed to get what he so desired was already—and had always been—within Him! He could do what he had been depending on others to do for him.

The moment he stopped looking for his strength in others and for his healing within the confines of the pool and people, he discovered a faith, which brought a change of focus. This, in turn, lifted him from his bed, and onto his feet! Miracles, wonders, dreams, and more, can happen when we allow faith to influence our focus!

This man found a change of focus and miracle-making faith! He found a faith that he did not know he had! It was a faith neatly packaged, but hidden behind his blurred vision and dependant attitude, a faith labeled, *I can do all things through Christ who strengthens me*! His power to effect a change in his life was within *him*—not with his peers, not in the pool, but within him! It was *his* faith that made him whole—*his* faith! For so many years he had looked, searched, and yearned for this change, only to find that the power to make it happen lay within him.

Many of us become trapped by our own outlook on life,

37

overly mindful of what we consider to be insurmountable life situations. Like the man at the pool, we feel helpless unless assisted, befriended, or loved by others; we consider ourselves inadequate, or less than good enough. Leaning on the whims and ever-changing emotions of people, our focus rests on our human *in*abilities rather than our God given-abilities.

God believes in you. He believes in you, despite what you, others, or circumstances say or portray. His belief in you will never be weakened by your lack of belief in yourself. He believes in you, because He knows you as no one else does. He knows exactly what you are capable of. Does anyone know the invention like the man or woman who invented it? I think not!

Listen to what Jesus said to the man, "Wilt thou be made whole?...Rise, take up thy bed and walk" (John 5: 6, 8). Jesus showed him that his healing had nothing to do with others, but everything to do with himself. He showed him that the choice was his: lie down lame or get up and walk. The lame man had the power to have what his heart so desired. You see, the power was in him—through faith! In other words, what Jesus was saying was that if you want it, you can have it! If you will, then you can, and he did!

After all those years of lameness, the man just got up and walked! There was no one there to hold his hand, no one to help pull him up, no one! He did it. He did it by faith changing-focus! He did it, and you can too!

My friend, it is in you! The faith you need for your miracle is in you. No excuse, no explanations—it is in you! Read the text and you will see where the man started giving Jesus the reason why he had not and why he could not, when really all Jesus was interested in was, "But do you *want* to?"

Start saying right now, "I can through Christ! I can through Christ! I can through Christ!" Doesn't it feel better than saying, "I can't?" Why is this? Because there is a power that God releases on your behalf when you begin to affirm the seemingly impossible things that can only be achieved through His strength. Now, if you would just for one moment stop telling yourself why you cannot and start telling yourself how you *can*, then your life will be transformed, right now, just as the lame man's was. Are you ready?

NOT MUCH, BUT ENOUGH

Do you know that even tiny faith can move a mountain and have it skipping into the sea? Isn't that astounding? Isn't it incredible? Many of us live our lives in the shadow of mountains because we think that we do not have a big enough or strong enough faith to shift them. But I want to tell you that you do not need large faith to move your mountain. It might sound strange at first. It did to me too when the Lord began to share this with me.

Listen to this: Jesus didn't ask us to have tons and tons of faith to witness a miracle; He just asked for faith the size of a mustard seed. Well, how big is a mustard seed? Small, incredibly small, so small in fact that if you were not careful you could easily hold it and not know it was in your hands.

This is indeed a hell-shaking concept! I know satan doesn't want you to get hold of it! But let me shout it into your consciousness: MUSTARD-SEED FAITH MOVES MOUNTAINS! Now this is a faith that you have! You can have it and not even recognize that you do because it is so small, and you are busy looking for something large!

Perhaps that is why the lame man didn't recognize that he could get up before he did!

One of the most beautiful things about God is that He doesn't make difficult what doesn't have to be. What He asks from us is nowhere near as much as what He is willing to give us in return. He will ask us for faith the size of a mustard seed (which is one of the smallest of the seed family, I might add) and then have that tiny, infinitesimal seedling of faith miraculously move something as colossal as a mountain. Surely the two do not equate! But then that is God.

Do you see? That is why we need a godly focus, to look beyond the bleakness of our situation to find a faith so small that it is easily overlooked in our blurred perception of what we see. Some of us are so busy trying to muster up a fiery-furnace faith when all our situation requires is a mustard-seed faith. Do not be fooled into thinking that the person who displays fire-in-the-furnace faith or lions'-den faith arrived there overnight, or without first planting, developing, and nurturing mustard-seed faith. Again I remind you that nothing is born fully grown. That is not the natural course of things. Roman 12:3 shows us that our measure of God-given faith can develop and grow, just like that of the mustard seed. Consider David, Israel's king-in-waiting; he would not have had the faith to overcome Goliath if he had not developed his faith, in his case, through the taking on of the bear and the lion, as a shepherd boy. If he had stepped out there in front of Goliath before his faith was tested on the bear and the lion, Goliath would have chewed him up and spat him out! Faith has to be developed and practiced. The lion and the bear were David's training ground or practice field in preparation for Goliath. God will allow circumstances to come your way so you can exercise your faith by putting it into practice, readying you for the purpose He has ahead of you.

The weight lifter does not immediately lift 350 lbs in weights—he works up to it over a period of time. What you and I so often fail to realize is that it is not that we do not have faith, but rather that we need it to grow. The disciples did not say to Jesus, after He told them how many times He expected them to forgive their brother in one day, "Give us faith," but rather, "Lord, *increase* our faith"—the operative word being *increase*. They recognized that they had faith, but felt they needed an *increase* to be able achieve what was expected of them. (See Luke 17:5.) Our level of faith is all we need to get us through the things we are going through! In essence you might be asking God to give you faith when you already have what you are asking for. He has given you a measure of faith. Now what you should be asking for is an *increase*.

What do you want to happen in your life? You have what it takes to make it happen. Catch hold of this: *it is in you*. What you are looking for *is in you*! That measure of God-given faith to turn your life around, to reach your goal, to overcome your struggles, to beat that habit, to kick that addiction, to break free from that destructive relationship, is *in you*!

Jesus gave the lame man a glimpse of the possibility available to him outside the confines of the pool—a possibility that had been with Him all the time. No one had ever challenged him to walk before, but this was his time for a change—his time for a miracle! Now I say to you that it is *your* time for a change. It is your time for a miracle! Seize the possibility.

CHAPTER 6

POSITIONED FOR PURPOSE, ON PURPOSE

MOSES WAS FORTY years old when His life took a turn, not for the worse but for the better. Fleeing from Pharaoh's wrath after murdering an Egyptian soldier, he must have been plagued by menacing feelings of negativity and by nagging questions such as, "What is happening to my life? Why is this happening to me?" And, "If only I'd...." But, yet unknown to Moses, a chain of events had been set in motion.

Thirsty and left to wander aimlessly through the desert, Moses must have thought that his life was wasted and finished. While sitting at a well, alone and without a friend in the world, Moses noticed some young ladies arriving at the well. As they drew from it, some shepherds began to stir up trouble with them, and Moses went to their aid. (See Exodus 2:15–17.)

After fighting off the shepherds, he was invited to meet Jethro, the young ladies' father. He later married Zipporah, Jethro's eldest daughter, and settled down to the peaceful, quiet life of a shepherd.

So here was Moses, moved from a beautiful palace of gold, ivory, and silk to the desert of sand, sheep, and seclusion. What a fall, some would say, but in the words of the cliché detective, "Did he fall, or was he pushed?" Based on the evidence before me, I would say it is conclusive: he was pushed.

Moses was en route for an appointment with destiny—an appointment with God. This was an appointment that was timetabled long before there ever was a Moses. If God had had need of a diary, His inscription might have read something like this:

Appointment with Moses
Place: back of Mount Sinai
Time: early
Agenda: Israel's deliverance

Moses' days of quiet married mountain life were coming to an end. He was carrying a promise of God that was of no use on a mountainside with sheep and stones. A struggling people were earnestly awaiting this promise of God—the fulfillment of God that would forever change the course of things!

Soon Israel would behold the tangible evidence of God's commitment to them in the person of Moses. Not Moses the prince or Moses the murderer, the coward, the shepherd or even Moses the recluse. You see, this was a totally different man, a man who had been eighty years in the making. This was Moses the deliverer, the personification of God's promise to Israel.

DESIGNED TO ORDER

As Moses stood on the banks of the mighty Red Sea after leading the children of Israel so victoriously out of Egypt, with millions of bewildered faces looking to him for a way of escape and the dread of Pharaoh's army hot on his trail, what was he to do? Quite frankly, to put it in popular terms, Moses was caught between a rock and a hard place. He didn't *know* what to do! Surely this was not where the Lord had led him! Perhaps he had made a wrong turn somewhere; perhaps he had not listened attentively enough to the directions God had given to him.

The proof that he was no longer in contact with God seemed blatantly obvious, in the form of the Red Sea! He had led God's people to a dead end; had Moses lost the plot? God would not lead His people to a dead end—or, would He? Yet, that is exactly what He did!

Listen, the Red Sea was God's idea! It had nothing to do with Moses making a wrong turn or misunderstanding what he heard. God had picked it! Yes, Moses was right on track. He did not reach the Red Sea haphazardly. He was led there! God designed everything!

The events that have occurred in your life have all been ordered and specifically designated for you. Did you know that? Not by one who hates you or wants to see you destroyed, but by One who loves you with an everlasting love and wants the very best for you—and that "One" is God Almighty! At times, when you are faced with adversity and those dead-end situations, you will find yourself questioning the very nature of your walk with God. But be assured, that *there is purpose in your position.* Even when it appears that things are going drastically wrong for you where you are, *there is a purpose in your position.* Even when every indicator opposes what God has told you or where He has sent you, hold on to Him! *There is purpose in your position.*

When God tells us to step out for Him, He has a way of holding some of the finer details back. He might show us the glorious end; but very rarely will God tell us about the difficult bits in between. No, He will not tell you about the Red Sea ahead of you or about Pharaoh's pursuing chariots of war. Why should He? He is not trying to frighten us to death.

It is so important that you do not let barriers and opposition cause you to lose faith in God. There might well be mammoth walls and barriers in your way, but barriers and obstacles cannot prevent God's work in your life! Indeed, one of their primary purposes is to give you the opportunity to witness Him moving them. What a testimony!

Don't you think that God could have opened up the Red Sea before Moses and the children of Israel got there? Of course He could, but then His children would not have had a testimony of His sea-moving power, and Moses would not have known the total confidence that God had vested in Him.

So, I say again, hold your position; put your focus wholly on God, stand still and see the salvation of the Lord. God is a purposeful deity; nothing happens to His children without a divine objective. Right now, you might be saying, "You mean all that has happened to me up to this point in my life has happened to me *on purpose*, with God allowing things to be the way they were, with God in control of it all? He actually *led* me here on purpose?"

Positioned for Purpose, on Purpose

Yes, you've got it! He is allowing it on purpose! But it is important that you understand that although it is all happening on purpose, that purpose is not a cruel one. Listen to what the Bible says, "The steps of a good man are ordered by the LORD: and he delighteth in his way" (Ps. 37:23). My friend, you may sometimes feel as though where you are is not where you are supposed to be, that God is not pleased with your current position, but the Word clearly shows that your walk has been well thought out and prepared by God, so stop fretting and just keep walking, you will be surprised to see where your steps will lead you. The Bible also says, "And we know that all things work together for good to them that love God, to them who are the called according to his purpose" (Rom. 8:28). Though your position may be painful, understand and believe that it is nonetheless purposeful. The devil wants you believe that you have it all wrong, that you are not suppose to be where you are right now, that you need to back track and start over again, with your head held down in shame. But how can you be in the wrong place when God has ordered your steps? Does God make mistakes? Friend you are where you supposed to be, and allow me tell you something else, where there is purpose there is power, and where there is power there is victory! The victory is yours! (The devil is a liar!)

So, standing on the brink of your Red Sea, backed up against a wall with no sign of a way out, is not evidence that God has left you, or that you have made a wrong turn somewhere along the way. On the contrary, it is overwhelming evidence that God is indeed *with* you. Would you know that you could exercise an authority to speak to your Red Sea if you were never confronted by it?

God's purpose will always prevail in spite of adverse

conditions. Can you imagine how crazy Moses must have looked and sounded to his fellow brethren when he stretched his rod over the Red Sea, shouting, "Stand still, and see the salvation of the LORD"? (Exod. 14:13). They must have thought, "We are following a madman!"

Perhaps you are in a bizarre place at this very moment, and you are wondering how and why you got there. If so, don't be afraid! Just stand still. God has your life ordered.

Only God would have the audacity to lead Moses and the children of Israel to an ocean as a way of escape, only God! But here is the beauty of it all. Not only will God lead you to an ocean, He will take you through it as well!

It is God and God alone, who has led you here, to this point in your life; and it has all been done on purpose! It has all been designed to order. God has drawn up the specifications, and it is He who has placed the order. Stand still and believe that you shall soon see the wonders the Lord will perform through your life, just as Moses did!

IT IS ALL RIGHT

We all hurt; we cry; we need help; we lose faith; we all feel lost at times. We do not understand sometimes; but amazingly, it does not matter. Often we struggle with the fear that people might find out that we are going through a difficult time. But Jesus, our greatest example, openly showed signs of His anguish in the Garden of Gethsemane.

The gospels reveal that as He carried the cross, He fell under its great weight. Because of the strain on Jesus, the soldiers commanded Simone of Cyrene to help Him, yes to help Him, to Help Jesus, the Messiah of the world!

See, some of us do not like to be helped or to ask for help. We find it difficult and sometimes embarrassing to show ourselves as anything but strong, and altogether, "I never find life difficult" folk. But when Jesus fell beneath His load, as we all do sometimes, He didn't think, "No I'm the Messiah, I can't fall or cry in front of these people; I can't show that the cross is too heavy for me!" No—He fell and He cried. He was not afraid or ashamed to show His emotions, whether it was pain, anger, sorrow, love, or anything else!

This type of selflessness can come only out of humility—the kind of humility that is not threatened or worried about being judged, that is not afraid of weakness or deterred by presumed shame. It is radiant in the face of adversity, shining its brilliant colors of love in a selfless display of beauty.

So unattractive are the beautiful garments of humility today. So enticing is the world's allure to trade them in for the ominous, deceptive garment of pride. Pride, which seeks not to show the slightest trace of pain, suffering or weakness, but rather to shelter its bearer from what it perceives to be the shame of suffering.

Like Indiana Jones in the film, *Raiders of the Lost Ark*, we can at times pretend to be unperturbed. For no matter what Indiana went through—quicksand, avalanches, mudslides, or fist fights—he always managed to emerge unruffled with his hat firmly fixed to his head. But our walk with God is not some entertaining stage show; it is real! A real walk with God will at times bring real pain, pain of which we need not be ashamed!

Jesus was never ashamed or embarrassed to show the disciples His pain. At one stage, He said, "My soul is exceeding sorrowful, even unto death," and then He asked for

His disciples help (Matt. 26:38). Matthew goes on to tell us that He "went a little further and fell on his face." And He pleaded in prayer, such was His anguish and struggle. Matthew could not have given us this vivid description of our Lord's anguish if He had not openly shown it. (See Matthew 26:39.)

It is all right to cry under the weight of your load. It is all right. You do not have to keep up appearances. Yes, there will be days when you just do not know what is happening to you, periods when you *think* you know, only to find yourself questioning what you thought you knew. Will God think any less of you for this? No!

Listen, when Herod threw John the Baptist into prison, John sent his disciples to ask Jesus, "Art thou he that should come, or do we look for another?" (Matt. 11:3).

John the Baptist, the forerunner of Jesus Christ, asked this question. John the Baptist, of whom Jesus said, "Among them that are born of women there hath not risen a greater than John the Baptist" (Matt. 11:11).

John, who as a babe in his mother's womb, leapt in recognition of Jesus—He was the one that cried, "Behold the Lamb of God, which taketh away the sin of the world" (John 1:29). The Gospels give us a clear account of him watching as Jesus stepped forward. It was John who heard the voice from heaven when He plunged Jesus into the Jordan to be baptized, and it was John who saw the heavens open and watched as a dove lighted upon Jesus' head.

John had spent his life's ministry testifying to Jesus' coming; yet, when the time came for him to push in faith and undoubting belief, he began to falter. He needed another affirmation—He needed Jesus' reassurance. Did Jesus send back an angry message, saying, "John you of *all* people should know better"? No, Jesus gave him the reassurance he needed. So if with John, how much more with you or I?

Why are we so afraid to show ourselves as we are? Why are we so reluctant to admit, even to ourselves, that a lot of the time we really do not know what God is doing until He decides to reveal it to us! Why do we feel that we have to have it all together, all the time, with all the answers?

I am not saying that we should be frightened, whimpering souls, but the truth is that there was not one coat of gloss covering the cross. It was heavy, rough, and painful then, and it still is now. Suffering is not easy. It makes no difference who we are, we all at one time or another go through suffering that feels unbearable, but do you know something? *It is all right.* Since your pain is real why shouldn't you be allowed to cry real tears? Do you know that there are some pains in our lives that warrant our tears? Yet still, we refuse to let them flow. But I have come to realize that there are some pains that we experience that we are going to have to cry over in order to get over.

How would it have been possible for Isaiah to tell us that Jesus was wounded and bruised, had Jesus covered up His wounds in embarrassment and shame? (See Isaiah 53:5.) There is no disgrace in being wounded, or bruised, or feeling the ache of this walk. Do you think that Moses had any idea of what to do when He was faced with the Red Sea? Was that to His discredit? Did it take anything away from who he was? Of course not, he showed us his vulnerability, yet how majestically strong he appeared.

When Peter saw Jesus out on the sea and decided to join Him, then after a while started to sink, did Jesus scold Him or did He lift Him? He lifted Him. (See Matthew 14:28.)

God knows what you are struggling with! Do not allow yourself to sink, when all you need to do is cry out to be lifted. Cry whenever you need to, regardless of who thinks it is inappropriate.

I am reminded of the man, Bartimaeus, who had a need— he wanted his sight. He heard that Jesus was passing his way, so he began to call out to Him. There were those who basically told him to shut up! But the Bible says that he cried all the more. He cried out until he was heard. Such was this man's cry that it stopped Jesus in His tracks. After all, what does it matter what people think of you when you bear a problem that so desperately needs solving, a wound that needs healing, a load that needs carrying? Only he knew the lonely darkness of his blindness, so why should he have been expected to remain piously silent in the face of healing? (See Mark 10:46.)

I remember, as a youngster of about age thirteen or fourteen, going out with three or four of my friends to another friend's house to eat our packed lunches. The school food hall was unable to accommodate us, as it was being refurbished. Anyway, while we ate there, my friend's mother kept offering us cakes, pasties, and other delicacies. Now, although I wanted to accept her offer of one more slices of homemade, freshly baked pineapple upside-down cake and light fluffy meat pasties, I never did. In all the times I visited his house, I only accepted her first offer, regardless of how much she insisted. I always declined, unable to overcome my fear of being seen as ill-mannered or impolite. But no such etiquette impeded my friend, Morry. The same age as me, he joined me each lunch time, as well.

Morry knew no taboo and no polite ritual! Every time

the opportunity arose, Morry would grab it and swallow it whole. No, Morry never left that home hungry or wishing he had eaten more! He would eat to his heart's content, declining nothing, eating everything.

One afternoon on our way back to school after a hearty lunch, unable to stand what I considered to be his rude and embarrassing behavior one moment longer, I asked Morry, as he munched on the remainder of a fresh cream cake he had picked up on the way out, "Boy, didn't your mother teach you any manners at all? Can't you ever say no? It's just not right, man!" He replied, "Listen, if you want to miss out on good food, just because you're trying to look pretty, that's your business, but don't expect me to join you!"

I learned a lesson that day: what is the point of putting on a show that looks good on the outside but feels empty on the inside? What is the point of placing your pride before your needs, of going hungry when a table is spread full with free food?

The blind man realized that an extraordinary opportunity was before him, within his reach——a chance to receive his sight. Refusing to remain blind another day just for the sake of good manners and propriety, he cried out as loudly as he could, "Jesus, thou Son of David have mercy on me." Those around him told him to be quiet, but the Bible declares that he cried out even more loudly. Like my friend Morry, he took advantage of the opportunity; he refused to allow it to pass him by.

So, I say again to you, just cry if you need to, you cannot score any brownie points with God by trying to show how tough you are because he knows you! He is not looking for tough people; He has no use for them. Sometimes being strong is about letting stuff out, not holding it in.

Don't Do It

When a group of cult followers and their leader were found dead somewhere in France, all lay out in their beds, their faces covered with purple triangle cloths. The media went into frenzy about the danger of cults and Christianity.

During the autopsies that followed, it was found that the leader of the group had been castrated. The inquest found out that he had struggled with homosexual tendencies for some time. Not wanting to address this plaguing imperfection, he had simply had himself castrated, then encouraged his followers to do likewise. But I am sure he found that being castrated did not take away what was tormenting him. I suspect it may have added further to his problem.

How many of us have taken or are taking unnecessarily drastic measures to ensure that our imperfections leave us alone or go unnoticed, simply because of our misguided perception of what God expects? Yes, the Word declares, "Ye shall be holy" (Lev. 20:26), but that holiness will never be attained through our own efforts!

We can never accomplish this holiness outside Jesus Christ. We are made holy *only* in Him. God knows everything there is to know about us. He knows every struggle that recurrently torments us, and He is able to give us the strength to overcome every single struggle!

Why hide from Him or pretend before Him? He is not an ogre; He is a Comforter! We cannot surprise Him. There should not be anything that we cannot tell him, and there is nothing that He cannot solve. It must grieve God to see us in torment, taking drastic measures to solve our own problems, when all we need do is call. I often tell my children that, no matter what they have done, regardless of how bad, they must not keep it from me. It will never make me love them any less or turn me against them. Now if I, an earthly mother, can feel that way about my children, why do we feel we have to put on a performance for God, or hide from Him, or not tell Him our shortcomings? He is our Father; He means us no ill. Give him what torments you; He has already appointed strength for you to overcome it! You do not have to mutilate your life or the life of your family because of what you are struggling with; do not isolate yourself from God! That is what the devil wants you to do. He wants you to mutilate your faith, your hope, and your trust. Instead, give God what ails you, and allow Him to gently heal you.

CHAPTER 7

THE CLOAK

ALL OF US, at times, feel that our lives are predictable and mundane, and that nothing appears to be happening to or *for* us. While others appear to be in the fast lane to success, we can seem to be in the slow lane to nowhere. But God has a way of placing us in the slow lane in order to bring out some very essential qualities in our lives.

You see, while the image of God is forming in us, it is necessary that He hide us away from the glare of the spotlight, for what artist of any standing carries out His work in the open?

I have come to understand that God has designed cloaks specifically for His children, to conceal them from the threats of the enemy, while He works on them—cloaks that have confounded satan so completely, time and time and time again. No one but God could design the cloaks that His children are covered with. They are so convincing that very few are able to detect the real person beneath them.

When Peter saw beyond Jesus' cloak and declared, to what must have been the astonishment of the other disciples, "Thou art the Christ, the Son of the living God" (Matt. 16:16), Jesus knew that Peter could not have seen what he saw without divine assistance. Jesus knew that God had whispered into the ears of Peter's spirit. That is why Jesus said, "Blessed art thou, Simon Bar-jo-na: for flesh and blood hath not revealed *it* unto thee, but my Father which is in heaven" (Matt. 16:17).

It is so important that we do not judge or label people based purely on what we see of them. For, as I have said before, God's kingdom does not operate by the earthly standard of "seeing is believing."

When the prophet Samuel was told by God to go down to the house of Jesse and anoint the next king of Israel, the prophet acted on what he could see through his natural eyes, not through the eyes of the Spirit. Samuel stood before the line of Jesse's handsome sons and made the same mistake that many of us make today in deciding whether we can or cannot be used by God: he looked at the outward appearance. (See 1 Samuel 16:6.)

He proclaimed, "Surely the Lord's anointed is before him." Then, he prepared to anoint Eliab, David's brother, as king. But God said to him, "Look not on his countenance, or on the height of his stature; because I have refused him: for the LORD seeth not as man seeth; for man looketh on the outward appearance, but the LORD looketh on the heart" (1 Sam. 16:7).

Before long, all of Jesse's sons had appeared before Samuel, except for David. So convincing was the cloak of the shepherd he wore that his father had not even bothered to call him, not thinking him to be a likely candidate for a king.

Let me tell you this: God, and God alone, truly knows who you really are. It will not merely be satan who will receive an incredible shock when God lifts the cloaks on some of His hidden children; there will be some who have treated God's children abusively who will be shocked as well.

The Bible tells an absolutely beautiful story in the book of Esther about the wondrous workings of God in the lives of his children. It is an account of God's ever-vigilant love and care for his children. It is an account of how He will do whatever it takes to keep us from being destroyed. God is on our side! He tells us over and over throughout His written Word that He is on our side, and no one and nothing can change this—no demons, no sickness, nothing.

The story involves a king (Ahasuerus), a Queen (Vashti), a cloaked, orphaned Jewish girl (Esther), a cloaked Jewish uncle (Mordecai), and an evil, conniving villain (Haman).

Now Haman made an ill-fated decision when He decided to callously take on God's children. He should have stayed well clear, when he stumbled upon Mordecai and Esther; he should have left them well alone. He did not realize that he was messing with the wrong people when he cruelly schemed to have all the Jews annihilated and Mordecai hanged.

He thought that Mordecai was a Jewish nobody, someone he could just wipe out at the drop of a hat, and that Esther was someone he could manipulate for his own evil purposes, but he was to find out how wrong he was! So sure was Haman of himself that he even went as far as building a gallows on which to have Mordecai hanged! But God had a very serious twist in this tale for Haman—one that He planned to reveal on Mordecai and Esther's unveiling day.

It was a day that would spell the beginning of the end for Haman. His murderous plans would backfire, and his heart would melt when God finished lifting the cloaks on his disguised children. Was he in for the shock of his life! The gallows, which he had specifically built for Mordecai, were soon to find Haman himself swinging from its noose!

Believe me, my friend, God always has a wondrous twist in the tale for the lives of His cloaked children. Haman conspired to kill a cloaked child of God, but God had other plans, as He always does. Never ever underestimate God!

Haman's demise is a very stark lesson that we need not be aroused or scared by people's perceptions or threatening acts towards us, for it is God who does the hiring and firing. He is the one who does the lifting up and the bringing down, the shutting and the opening, and it is He who ultimately lifts our cloaks on our unveiling day. What a day!

HE HAS YOU CLOAKED

Take a look with me at what heaven called Gideon—*a mighty man of valor.* (See Judges 6:12.) Oh, come on, a mighty man of what? *Valor?* Hold on a minute! Didn't Gideon spend most of His life in fear and servitude, defeat and humiliation? Isn't it true that all he seemed to be good for was running and hiding? Why would heaven refer to him in this way? Well, the answer can be found in the cloak!

Listen to how Gideon responds when God gives to him his commission of delivering Israel, "Oh my Lord, wherewith shall I save Israel? Behold, my family is poor in Manasseh, and I am the least in my father's house." Gideon thought of himself and his family as nothing, not realizing that he was not what his circumstances were saying about him! This man who saw himself as insignificant and perhaps even rather pathetic was being referred to as "mighty" by heaven! Heaven can make no mistakes! If it calls you *mighty, great, beloved,* or *more than a conqueror,* then that is exactly what you are!

Every time I think about the cloak, I am thrilled. There are so many of God's sons who are cloaked right now, who are out there not knowing who they really are. I would even dare to say that if this book is in your hands, you too are one of the ones whom God has cloaked.

Perhaps you have been struggling with your life up until now, with who you are and where you think you should be. God wants you to know and trust in what He is doing. He has not forgotten or forsaken you. He has merely cloaked you.

The cloaked years are an essential time, but they are also a time of virtual obscurity—a time of development and transformation, of growth in wisdom, stature, and favor, with both God and man.

Look at God's concealing, imaginative genius: He disguised a king in the cloak of a shepherd boy—David; a prince in the cloak of a trickster—Jacob; a mighty prophet in the cloak of a sycamore gatherer—Amos; a queen in the cloak of an orphaned Jewish girl—Esther; and greatest of all, the Savior of the world in the cloak of a carpenter's son—Jesus!

Who would have thought that a little shepherd boy would become the greatest earthly king of Israel? Or, who would have thought that the lowly son of a carpenter would be the Savior of the world? Truly, the workings of Almighty God are beyond comprehension. God's heavenly wardrobe is packed with all sorts of outfits, made to measure, specifically for His people, outfits to cover visionaries, pioneers, apostles, intercessors, and many more!

Let me tell you that God will hide you in the cloak of a broken wife or husband; hide you in the cloak of a criminal, a reckless drifter, an addict, a down-and-out nobody, and then suddenly, at an appointed time, He will shock and amaze you and your world by unveiling the *real* you.

Now consider this, does God have you cloaked?

Blowing Your Cover

To blow one's cover is to reveal one's true identity before the time. So we need a firm discipline to enable us to walk with the knowledge of the call of God on our lives and still be willing to wait for God to reveal it in His time.

Many of us need only to know that God has called us, for us to be wanting to get out there and get things done, even though we are as yet ill-equipped for the task we wish to tackle. No one had more reason to blow His cover than Jesus. He was the Messiah! He could have said, "I'm the Savior of the World! I am not a carpenter's son! I've come to save the world, not to sit around mending chairs! I'm out of here!" But He submitted to hiding himself under the cloak until it was time for Him to be revealed.

Jesus knew who He was and what He had come to do, and He knew this from an early age. There was an incident when He was so eager to do the work of His heavenly Father that He left His parents' side, and was found three days later in a temple, holding a discussion with the professional men of the day. They were astounded at the level of His understanding because He was only twelve years old at the time. (See Luke 2:48–49.)

When His parents found Him, they must have been at their wits' end, especially His mother. It was natural that they would ask Him where He had been and what He had been doing. But He calmly replied, "I was about my father's business" (v. 49, author's paraphrase) and at that moment, they must have caught a glimpse of who was under the cloak. Jesus had to pull it quickly back in humble submission to their will, so as not to expose Himself before the appointed time. It was not yet time for Him to reveal Himself; He was not ready yet, even though He was dazzling the men of renown with his knowledge (v. 47). He still was not ready, and He was in danger of blowing His cover.

It seems strange to think that Jesus was not yet ready to fulfill the purpose for which He came. But it is true: He was not ready.

It was not God's right time for Him. Move before your time and you will be ill-prepared for the task God is preparing you for, and the people to whom God is calling you will be ill-prepared to receive you. You must possess the strength of humility, to know who you are and yet subject yourself to staying under God's cloak.

The Word says of Jesus, "And he went down with them" (Luke 2:51). *Them* refers to His parents. Jesus, the Savior of the world, the Emmanuel, the Lamb that was slain from the foundation of the world, had to submit himself to the will of His earthly parents so that the designed purpose of the cloak could effectively work for His good. (See Luke 2:51.)

Submission is not a word that we swallow easily; the reason for this is that we attempt to swallow it without love. Love is like the water you take to help the pill go down. Submission outside of love is not the submission God asks of us. In fact, it is defeat. Nevertheless, for the cloak to have God's desired effect, you and I must learn the lesson of submission and learn it well. If you are struggling with where you are right now perhaps what you need to do is simply to go down, abase yourselves, and submit, for the sake of the call of God on your life.

It was eighteen years before we heard anything of Jesus again! Eighteen years of total silence. There must have been times when He was bursting with power, with revelations to share, but He had to hold his peace. Eighteen years of submission—now that is what you call discipline, humility, and submission!

So God has told you that you are going to be a mighty preacher of His Word, or that you going to contribute greatly to His kingdom? Acquire an understanding of the call's timing. Is it really now? Or is it *you* who are wanting it, forcing it to be now?

Go back under the cloak, my friend. All of your eager, uncontrolled zeal is about to blow your cover. Don't you know that the cloak is there to throw the enemy off your scent?

It has become very apparent to me over the years that those who blow the loudest trumpets about who they are and what they are capable of, are the ones who are no more ready than Peter was when He told Jesus that He would never leave Him, but die with Him. It seems to me that there is a humble, undisturbed quietness that comes with godly readiness.

No good craftsman will reveal a work of art that is half-finished. Allow God to do the revealing; He will know when you are ready to be uncovered.

I AM NOT MY CLOAK

Can you imagine the consequences of Jesus' believing in the cloak of a carpenter's son? The entire world would be in a permanent state of complete darkness. Our lives depended on Jesus believing in and moving in His calling when the time was right for Him to do so, thus fulfilling His purpose.

Jesus was not born to be a carpenter—this was merely His cloak. If you allow yourself to believe in the disguise and take it on, so to speak, so that it becomes the real you, you will never receive anything that God is doing in your life, no matter how great it is! You will always dwell in the carpenter's shop, among the sawdust and wood chippings. Your talk will always be wooden, inanimate, and dull, instead of animated and powerful.

You will always dwell on the cloak and not on who is being formed under it. When hardship occurs in your life, you will interpret it as being your lot and give up, instead of understanding that it is just the process in operation.

How often have you seen people getting carried away with the cloak covering an artist's painting or sculpture? They do not visit the gallery to look at the cloak, but rather the work of art beneath the cloak!

The cloak is not designed to fool you! It is there to give God time to accomplish His work in you, to fool the enemy into believing you are an unimportant nobody, no threat to Him at all.

So you see, it is essential that you embrace what God is

doing in your life, in trusting, humble submission. God has you hidden in divine obscurity in order to form you. The cloak He has covered you in will make sure that the enemy will not even give you a second glance. By the time He gets wind of who you really are, it will be too late; you will be long gone!

This reminds me of the incident in the tomb, when Jesus unveiled one of His cloaks. As He lay there in the tomb for three days and three nights, the enemy was rejoicing. Indulge in my imagination for one moment, if you will.

I imagine that on the last night, just before Jesus rose, the enemy might have laughingly said, "Can you imagine after all His declarations of power and Lordship that He's still lying in the tomb dead? Didn't He say that He was going to get back up again on the third day? And isn't this the third day? What victory, we've won!"

But no sooner had the words left his mouth than he hears a movement coming from inside the tomb. Rushing in to see what could be going on, they witnessed Jesus rising up and shrugging off His cloak. The glory of the eternal Creator, God, shone forth and lit up the very depths of hell. Stepping forward, Jesus, His voice more powerful than the one that cried from the cross, declared, "O death, where is thy sting, O grave, where is thy victory?" (1 Cor. 15:55). With the smile wiped so completely from his countenance, all satan and his agents could do was bow.

Many of us are either ripping at our cloaks or becoming overly indulgent with them. We need to stop, for with every blow of God's divine hammer on the chisel and every rub of His sandpaper, we are being made into His glorious image.

From this point onwards, look at yourself and your life

differently by using the knowledge of the cloak, and know this: God will never present you until you are ready. When God lifts that cloak off you, you will be more than ready for the task for which you were born.

THOUGHTS OF THE SCULPTURE

At the end of a long day, when the lights in the artist's workshop are switched off and the doors are locked, the sculpture is once again covered by the artist's cloak. Its thoughts might seep out from under the covering.

"Gosh it's dark under here, and kind of lonely too. I never get out for long, always having to be covered."

(Silence.)

"I wonder if the master knows what he's doing. All that hammering and chiseling seems to be lasting forever and it's really hard to stay covered all the time, especially when I catch a glimpse of myself in the mirror. I look good; it must be time for me to come out now!"

(Silence.)

"There are so many other sculptures around me that are already worked on and out; it doesn't seem fair. I wish..."

(Silence.)

"They're out there in the gallery, but look at me, look where I am. I don't know that I will ever be ready; just when I think I am, he starts chiseling away at something else on me."

(Silence.)

God's grand, well-thought-out, carefully planned cloak is so convincing, it even has *you* mystified, but stay put—He knows what He is doing!

CHAPTER 8

STORMY WEATHER

LOOKING BACK TO the morning when I awoke to a spiritual storm that was to herald a season of extreme pain and great struggle for me, I do not remember receiving any warnings about an approaching storm. There were no seriously dark clouds, no claps of thunder or lighting. Life was a blue sky, with a few dark days—nothing I could not handle. Then suddenly, as if from nowhere, the serenity that I thought was characterizing my life was gone in a moment.

I felt so unprepared! For, what do you do when a storm blows up your tranquility and shatters all of your hopes and dreams? What do you do when everything you have prayed and lived for is swept away by a storm? But perhaps the question should not really be about what *you* do, but rather about what has, is, and will be done, by whom and why? When you find the answers to these questions, which I will help you to do through this chapter, you will find peace in the midst of the storm.

Overnight my ability to pray and see its results was gone, blocked. My connection seemed severed: *where was God?* My usual form of worship and praise lost its passion in my confusion and distress, and, try as I might, it appeared that I just could not find God! Have you ever been there? Have you ever prayed, but you could not feel Him? Have you ever called and He did not answer you? You looked, and He was nowhere to be seen? When you longed for a night vision to reassure you that everything was all right and that He was still with you, but nothing? When you looked in all the usual places of praise, prayer, fasting, reading, and meditating on the Word, but you still could not find Him? Have you ever felt that you had lost Him? That He had left you? That you were separated from your God? Well that is where *I* was, and it was sometime during this period that God silently used an incident with a bus to teach me about where I was in my life. I call it the *believer's blind spot.*

BLIND SPOTS

How can one lose and be unable to find an omnipresent God—a God who fills all time and space? The answer to this question can be found in the *believer's blind spot,* so read on and I willl explain exactly what I mean.

Most experienced drivers know that there is a blind spot in the wing mirrors of a vehicle. So sightless is this spot that you could, quite easily, unknowingly, miss or lose something as large as an articulated lorry or a double-decker bus. What I mean by this is that the lorry or the bus can be there, but you do not see it in your mirror because of the mirror's blind spot.

The disclosure of this blind spot occurred one morning as I hurried to work in my car. Rushing towards a major junction, anxious to get to my destination, I checked my mirror before moving out onto this extremely busy junction, but did not bother to glance over my shoulder, to see if there was anything there. Pulling out, I was confident that the way was clear and that there was nothing beside or approaching me. Then I heard the alarming sound of a horn, and, looking across, to my utter amazement, there almost on top of my car was a double-decker bus, as large as life! I was totally shocked! Where had it come from? It was not there when I checked my mirror. It seemed impossible to think that I could have missed something as huge a bus, but I had! Why? Because I did not know about the driver's blind spot. I did not know that when overtaking or making any such maneuver, as well as checking your mirror for oncoming traffic, you also need to glance over your shoulder, as the shoulder glance gives a truer vision of what is really there!

I began to relate my experience with the bus to our walk with God. For, of a truth, there are times when He appears not to be around, times we just cannot see Him. But I have come to understand that all of us have blind spots in our lives, angles from which we are unable to see God, positions from which He appears not to be there, although He *is there*.

Job experienced *the believer's blind spot* when He was being attacked by the devil. God appeared not to hear his cries or even be around to deliver him. Job cried out to find God. He was looking for God in the usual way and in the usual places, but God just did not appear to be there. Job just could not find Him! He said, "Oh that I knew where I might find him! that I might come even to his seat!" (Job 23:3). "Behold, I go forward, but he is not there; and backward, but I cannot perceive him: On the left hand, where he doth work, but I cannot behold him: he hideth himself on the right hand, that I cannot see him" (Job 23:8–9). How could he not see someone as large and omnipotent as God? The blind spot. Job could have, like me at the junction, moved on the basis of what he *could* see; yet, he decided not to. Instead he declared, "If a man die, shall he live again? all the days of my appointed time will I wait, till my change come" (Job 14:14). What do you do when you cannot find God? You wait.

The danger of the believer's blind spot is that we will be tempted to move on what we can see from its blinkered position. Job realized that although he could not find God, God knew exactly where he was. So instead of moving, he declared that he would stay right where he was and wait. A decision made based on one's vision from this position will inevitably be the wrong one.

David in the psalms wrote, "Surely goodness and mercy shall follow me all the days of my life" (Ps. 23:6). David could say this with all confidence, because he had faced many blind spots in his life. He had faced times when he outright struggled to find God. However, somehow the eyes of his faith glanced over the shoulders of his soul, there only to see the lover of his soul—God covering His back, preparing a table for Him in the presence of His enemies. In that moment, David experienced God anointing his head with oil until His cup was so full that it ran over. (See Psalm 23:5.)

Had I glanced over my shoulder before I pulled out that day, I would have seen the bus right beside me. Faith is a glance. It helps you to see what would have otherwise been hidden. A whole new picture emerges when the believer takes a glance of faith, for faith is evidence of the invisible. The glance of faith will make all the difference! With faith, black and white becomes color; that which was far off suddenly becomes near; and that which was too fantastic to accept becomes real enough to believe, touch, and handle. A glance of faith, over the shoulders of the believer's soul, will change partial sight to complete, limitless vision. How wondrous it is to know that the God we believed to be far off is so much closer than we could ever have of imagined had it not been for faith's glance.

PURPOSE IN THE STORM

Storms can be so destructive especially when their root instigator is the enemy. However, in saying this, I recognize that God can and *will* use the destructive plans and activities of satan to fulfill His purposes. Our attention, therefore, should not be given so much to the instigator of the storms to his destructive intentions, as to the ruler of all storms, God.

When Jesus was on board the ship with His disciples, satan blew up a storm while He slept. Note that satan caused the storm only when he knew Jesus was sleeping. Satan will always attempt to take you out of heaven's reach when he considers you to be at your most vulnerable. Always remember that! Jesus and His disciples were in the middle of the sea; Jesus was sleeping at the bottom of the ship. What an opportunity—one not to be missed! I might add that the devil is quick to maximize and to exploit every opportunity.

The disciples panicked, not knowing how to combat the ferocity of the storm. So they cried to Jesus, "Master, carest thou not that we perish?" (Mark 4:38). They could not understand how Jesus was able to sleep in such a life-threatening situation. But Jesus calmly arose and took authority over the storm, rebuking the wind and speaking peace to the waves. He immediately recognized that satan was trying to kill Him at sea before He could accomplish His mission. Notice that He rebuked the wind, not the sea. He did this because He recognized the prince of the power of the air was within its gust. Oh we have to know what to rebuke and when! Whenever satan seeks an occasion to destroy, God always uses his attempts as an opportunity to demonstrate His sovereignty.

So Jesus rebuked this physical storm, and, yet, we note that He did not move against the metaphorical storm which rose up against Him in the murderous hearts of the scribes and the Pharisees. Why? Why didn't He rebuke them and quell the storm in these cruel men, just as He did when He was at sea? Because He knew that the storm of their murderous intentions was in accordance with His ultimate purpose, His destiny. The hate-filled storm of the Pharisees and scribes, like the wave that carries the surfer along, or the cloud that carries the rain, would deliver Jesus to His destiny. So there was no way that He was going to rebuke *this* storm, even though He knew it would carry Him to His death. Even though Jesus had the power to rebuke it and stop it, He restrained himself for the sake of His ultimate purpose. In that very essence lies the deciding factor of how we approach our storms—whether we know our purpose.

If you have a clear understanding of your purpose, it will enable you to resist and rebuke those situations that seek to hinder or prevent the fulfillment of that purpose, regardless of how painful that situation is. We never once read in any of the gospels that Jesus rebuked or resisted Judas' traitorous intentions towards Him even though He clearly knew what they were. He even told Judas to do whatever he was going to do quickly. So why didn't Jesus resist Judas and tell the other disciples of Judas' evil plan? Why didn't Jesus simply confront and challenge Judas, or make him change his mind? Because He knew that Judas's actions were ushering Him towards His divine purpose on earth. Jesus even went as far as referring to Judas as "friend" during his act of betrayal in the garden of Gethsemane. Neither do we hear Jesus begging to be taken down from the cross, although He was consumed with pain and feelings of rejection. Why? Because He had accepted His purpose and the imminent pain and reproach it would bring.

The reason we struggle so much with the storms in our lives is possibly because we do not yet know our purpose, so we are unable to differentiate one storm from another. We judge every storm as one to be rebuked, only seeing satan in its claps of thunder, rather than God in its mighty gusts. But when we truly begin to accept that God has every area of our lives covered, and that He is watchful in the most loving way over every breath we take, and careful of our every move, we will begin to see our purpose and consequently find confidence in the midst of any storm. We will allow it to run its course, despite being unsure of its consequences, knowing that we will emerge having achieved our purpose in God. Our poise in the storm is determined by our recognition of what God's purpose is for us; we will either be fretfully rebuking or confidently restful.

DESPITE THE STORM

The account of Peter's walk of faith on the sea shows us that God will bid you to come to Him in the midst of your storm, but not necessarily bid the storm to cease. He will call you to His service right in the middle of your upside-down, storm-tossed situation.

Many people hear the call of God in their lives but fail to respond because they are waiting for their circumstances to get better. They wait for their personal storm to die down. But the mere fact that God's call has come during the storm means that He expects you come, *regardless*. More often than not, the storm will not die down, but God wants us just to step out, regardless of the elements.

When Jesus bade Peter to come to Him, the wind was whistling about Peter's head, and the waves were beating up against his boat. But still, Jesus said, "Come!" (Matt. 14:29). He didn't say, "Come, but don't step out of the boat just yet; wait there for a moment! Let me calm the wind and the waves for you first." No, Jesus wanted Peter to step out of the boat into the choppy storm-churned sea, and Peter took that incredible step of faith; He stepped out of the boat and onto the water. Surely, at seeing such a momentous step of faith, Jesus would now cause the wind and the waves to cease, but no, He allowed them to continue. Peter, undeterred, continued to walk on the water, until he took his focus off Jesus and placed it on the boisterous waves and the contrary winds. At this point Peter began to sink.

There are two lessons here: the first is that as long as we are overly considerate of our stormy situations, we will never find the courage or the faith to step out of the boat. We will always remain "boat-bound Christians," scared and paralyzed by our storms. We will never know the trust, faith, and focus of the *water walker*. The second issue is that it is focus, trust, and faith in God and His power to uphold us that will allow us to move beyond our circumstances and enable us to remain above the water, in the midst of the storm. If you allow your focus to dwell on the storm, then that is all you will ever see, but if your focus is Jesus, you will find courage bigger than any storm you face.

Understand then that the call of God is not given to us because our lives are storm free or squeaky clean. God knew the condition of our lives long before he bade us come; He bids us, despite it. No one else but God would take someone out of a stormy life and give them responsibility; His call comes in the midst of your upheavals. Why? Because He wants us to know that we can rise above anything. If we put our trust, faith, and love in Him, we will walk *on* water and not be drowned *in* it.

So get up from where you are right now and start responding to His bidding, focus on *Jesus*, not on the storm. You will see that, as you begin change your focus, the storm that has been blowing through your life will not necessarily die down. But just as Jesus did, you will rise above it. Things do not seem as bad when you can get on top of them.

God will call you despite your storm, despite your problems, your pain, and your grief; His call is greater than any storm you face. I can say this because I have stepped out of my boat with the storm blowing about my head in answer to His call. To say that it has been easy would be to mislead you. There have been many times when, like Peter, I became aware of the waves about my feet, times when I took my focus from God, but as a colleague once told me when I was leaving my job for ministry, "Bev, God is able."

I remember when my daughter first began to walk. How many times she would take her focus from me and fall to the ground with a bump! How she would cling to the furniture, using it as her support as she clambered around the room. Every now and then she would let go for a second or two, and then losing her balance she would grab hold of the furniture again. Then she would let go and take a few more intrepid steps across the room, her confidence in her ability to walk unaided growing with each step.

One day, responding to my beckoning, she let go of the sofa and took several small but sure steps across the room to me. She was so focused, balanced, and determined. Then, suddenly, as though realizing what she was achieving, she lost her concentration and came crashing to the floor. But do you know something? For every step she made, no matter how small, I praised her. When she fell, I picked her up in my arms, held her tight, and hugged her, each time setting her back on her feet and again beckoning her to come. I knew she would do it one day, and she did!

Our walk with God is not so different from that of my daughter. We are all at different stages, with many obstacles and trials facing us, but God, the one who bids us come, has boundless patience, love for, and confidence *in* us to accomplish what He calls us to do. It does not matter how many times we get it wrong, how often we fall, or cling on to external supports. He knows that our intention is to walk, to come, to respond to His beckoning. So He lifts us when we are sinking and carries us when we are weak. When we cannot take any more, He comforts and encourages us and calls us His beloved. He reminds us that He is our loving Father.

There were definitely times during my storm when I felt I would never make it through, when all my instincts were telling me to get back into the boat. There were times when I lost my focus and became so conscious of my storm that nothing existed beyond or above it, particularly when it grew more and more severe and appeared to have no end. But God was not as concerned about my making sense of the storm as much as He was about my finding faith to trust Him through it, and somehow I did! And you will too!

IT MUST BE ACCOMPLISHED

Consider this for one moment: there is a Word that God has spoken about your life that must come to pass because it has already proceeded out of His mouth. Because He cannot lie, that Word will never change. Now you may not agree with, like, see, or even believe this Word, but nothing will impede, deter, or nullify His Word. What proceeded out of the mouth of God concerning you, perhaps years ago, is what He will stand by until it has accomplished the purpose for which it was sent. It makes no sense fighting or running away from it, for no matter where you go, it will find you time and time again. The Word of God is like oil floating on the surface of water; it will not sink or go away. Its way is through *you*; you are its vehicle of accomplishment! So stand still and allow it to come to pass.

As the ingredients of bread have to go through a process of blending, folding, beating, and finally intense heat before they can become the finished product, so you will have to go through a process before you can become God's finished product. When the Word reaches you, it immediately begins to work in you: from Word believed, to

Word received, to Word conceived, and finally to Word achieved. This evolution of God's Word in your life is no easy accomplishment. Remember what the Virgin Mary said when she was told by the angel that she would bear a child, "How shall this be, seeing I know not a man?" (Luke 1:34). The angel explained it and then Mary said, "Be it unto me according to thy word" (Luke 1:38). Immediately after she said this, she conceived. Can you see the progression of God's Word in her? Believed, received, conceived, and finally after forty weeks achieved!

However, be warned that, for the most part, believing, receiving, conceiving, and bringing to fruition a word from God cannot happen without faith. This is because his word will often go against the very core of your human understanding and what you deem to be logical, sensible, and sane. After all, who would have believed that a virgin could conceive without intimate relationship with a man?

God's Word of purpose will challenge you to the very core of your walk with Him, rock your safe and secure place, speak of much more than you will be able to see in the here-and-now, and comprehend in the ever-and-ever, outside of faith. Nevertheless, do not doubt what you thought you heard God say just because it sounds like an unattainable enigma. You are serving a God who will tell you that you are going to be a pastor when you are closer to the exit sign of the church than you are to the pulpit; who will tell you are going to be the dean of a Bible school when you spent barely enough days at school to have your name registered; who will tell you that you are going to have a worldwide ministry when the one you already have is struggling to walk, let alone fly.

From my experience, it is when He speaks like this to

us that we are tempted to run and hide as Saul did when he was about to be anointed the first king of Israel. What you have to understand is that often what God has told you today will not be visible in the now; and, therefore, it is very possible that there will be no tell-tale signs to corroborate His words to you. Imagine for one moment how hard it must have been for Mary to believe God's words. She could only receive it all through faith.

When Jesus met Peter and called him to be His disciple, He told Peter that he would make him a fisher of men. "Hence forth thou shalt catch men" (Luke 5:10). Now no one could argue that, at that moment, Peter was ready for the task expected of him. He was unusable and unrefined, and so he had to undergo a change before that word could be fulfilled in his life. Later we hear Peter declare of Jesus, "Thou art the Christ, the Son of the living God" (Matt. 16:16), but this was by no means proof that he was ready for service, even though Peter might have thought so himself.

Jesus told him that He was going to give him the keys of the kingdom of heaven, the authority and power to loose and to bind. (See Matthew 16:19.) But still we see Peter go on to make blunder after blunder. The years passed by from the time when Jesus had first spoken into Peter's life; yet still Peter was proud, impulsive, strong-minded, and strong-willed, so much so that He challenged Jesus' word on several occasions. What was happening? Hadn't Jesus spoken a word on His life? Yes he had, but Peter was in transition; he was still in the process of becoming who Jesus said he would be.

Time went on and still there was no visible evidence in Peter's attitude to validate the prophetic word that Jesus had spoken of him, not the slightest bit of proof that he could be anything other than an impulsive, obstinate know-it-all. Peter, after his shameful denial of Jesus, fled back to his former profession of fishing. Yes, the kingdom key-holder, of all people, fled! But God was not through with him, although he may have been through with himself! God's word had been spoken, and it had to accomplish its purpose in Peter's life.

Do not ever write off a word spoken by God on your life because you do not see yourself fitting the profile. It does not really matter what *we* can or cannot see, feel or do not feel, but only that *God* has spoken! That *God* has said it!

Then, on the Day of Pentecost, the word that Jesus had spoken on Peter's life all that time before finally came into its own. You have to understand that there are some things that God will say which will arrive tomorrow, but there are others that take a little longer. The main thing is that, whether it is a short time coming or a long time coming, it *will* come. Now here on the Day of Pentecost we see a completely transformed Peter. This was a new Peter, who was through with running scared, being proud, being impulsive; a new Peter who was now unafraid of people's opinions, or favor; a new Peter, standing firm amidst jeering and mockery; not with his old mind, or out of his own strength or arrogance, but with a fully renewed mind. Standing with the authority of a kingdom key-holder, to declare the Word of God to a mocking crowd with such power and passion that 3,000 souls were saved that day; at last the "kingdom key-holder" was born! (See Acts 2:14.) At last the cloaked fisherman was unveiled as heaven's "kingdom key-holder."

Trust God, my friend, trust him, even when it makes no sense at all, and when all you can see in your life is contrary to the word he has spoken to you. Still trust. Not one of God's words spoken to you will ever fall to the ground.

Perhaps you have lost hope because you could not see happening in your life or circumstances what God said would happen. You have moved away when you really should have stayed. But let me just say this: whatever it is that you have given up hope on or moved away from, if God has spoken to you about it then you are going to find you have to go back to it; you have to because God's word must and *will* come to pass. He never starts anything He is not going to finish; He never speaks anything that will not come to pass.

WEATHER-CHANGERS

My workplace, which had been such a blessed place for me, became an absolute nightmare when my boss, with whom I had built a great working relationship, left and was replaced by a woman who absolutely hated me from the moment she met me. She worked relentlessly against me in a hellish campaign to make my life miserable.

My previous boss had enabled me to fit the job around my family commitments, but this woman would have none of it. She stopped all the privileges I had accrued over my ten years of service, such as flexi-time, company car, emergency leave, etc. She lied about me many times and set colleagues and other managers against me. It was a rough time.

We often think that because we respond to the call of God, things will be rosy and shiny around us; all our problems will melt away, and everything will be wonderful. Well, to a certain extent I admit that I thought that way too. But I found it to be an extreme exception, certainly not the rule.

Have you ever felt sure of what God was doing in your life, of what He was calling you to do? But on stepping out, you found that things started going wrong, absolutely haywire? All of a sudden people started lying about you, running you down, fighting you at every possible opportunity; friends turned into enemies, and enemies appeared as friends. You found yourself right in the middle of a storm, a storm you had thought would cease because you had stepped out.

All at once, the confidence and strength you thought you had lay in ruins, broken and bruised. Stepping out for God does not seem so exciting any more; it is nothing like what you heard preached to you day-in and day-out. You begin to question yourself and your ability to do what you thought God told you to do. You were looking for things to change for the better when you showed up on the scene, but instead, everything just got worse, and kept going that way. Feeling let down, discouraged, confused, and alone, you could not help but ask the question, "God, what is happening? I thought you said...!" Well, do you know something? I believe that was how many of the patriarchs, prophets, apostles, and believers of old must have felt!

Take Moses, for example. After he responded to God's call to tell Pharaoh to "let my people go," I do not think that in his wildest dreams he could have anticipated the storm that he activated when his feet touched Egyptian soil. After all, the message seemed simple enough, but I have come to understand that often the simpler the message, the more the opposition. If you do not agree, just look at how simple Jesus' messages were, and then look at the conflict that ensued.

Pharaoh became so angered by Moses' requests from

God that he commanded the children of Israel, who were then Egypt's slaves, to have no further supplies of straw to make bricks! Instead, they were to gather the straw for themselves. And, as if that were not enough, they were still expected to produce the same quota of bricks as before!

It was an unachievable task. The officers set up as taskmasters over the children of Israel were repeatedly beaten for not accomplishing it. Things just could not get much worse. What was this? Didn't God say, "Go and tell Pharaoh to let my people go"? Then why all this? Why the storm?

Moses struggled to understand what was happening because he had done everything God had asked of him. He had followed his instructions, yet it seemed that the children of Israel were better off without him and his messages! Listen to what Moses says to God after he was attacked and blamed by the officers for their increased pain and labor, "Lord, wherefore hast thou so evil entreated this people?" (Exod. 5:22). It sounds to me as if he is rather angry, dejected, and disappointed with God! "Why is it that thou hast sent me? For since I came to Pharaoh to speak in thy name, he hath done evil to this people; neither has thou delivered thy people at all" (Exod. 5:22–23).

Perhaps Moses had had an image of how everything was going to take place when he got down to Egypt. However, events did not measure up to what he had pictured in his mind! Perhaps Moses had expected that, immediately upon hearing his words, Pharaoh would fall down in submission, servitude, and awe of him. Then he would simply stroll out of Egypt with the all the people of Israel and their belongings. God would be at his side, and the people would be in love with him, hailing him a hero. Perhaps that was his image of how it would be—an image with no resistance, no storm, and certainly no pain! But this did not happen! Instead, the people scorned Him *and* God. God appeared not to have kept His side of the bargain! The situation seemed much worse than before he arrived! Moses felt confused and bewildered. I believe that it was natural for him to assume that, after stepping out for God, things would all run smoothly.

However, from my case studies (Moses being one of them) and from my own experiences, I have discovered that this presumption is so far from the truth that it is almost laughable. Our acceptance of God's call to our lives does *not* negate the storm, but rather ignites it. We are the will of God on earth, and our presence in any given situation will cause one of two reactions in people: either great love, trust, and calm, or mistrust and hatred. Moses received the latter from Pharaoh, and occasionally even from factions among the children of Israel. Do not always expect folk to love you just because you stretch out a hand to help them!

Being in Jesus Christ makes us weather-changers; we affect the atmosphere! Sometimes things will appear fine until we turn up on the scene. Remember the man in the synagogue, who was possessed? I believe that he visited that place daily and sat undisturbed, perhaps even unnoticed by the people who frequented the synagogue. Then one day Jesus, the weather-changer, walked in. The Bible tells us that the moment Jesus entered, the demon cried out, "Let us alone; what have we to do with thee, thou Jesus of Nazareth? art thou come to destroy us? I know thee who thou art, the Holy One of God" (Mark 1:24). Jesus changed the atmosphere! He brought life to the place—and with it, His light, warmth, heart, love, and truth, all of which changed the atmosphere! Believe me when I say that demons know when you are in town!

Remember King Herod? He flew into a murderous rage when he heard that a child was born to be the king of the Jews. He ordered the merciless slaughter of hundreds of Hebrew babies, hoping that he might kill the special babe.

Jesus was a baby, so what possible threat could he be to Herod? The only thing He had done was to be born. But that was enough to cause a storm in the heart of the king, in the courts of the palace, and in the streets of Jerusalem. His presence alone was enough to change the weather.

It is clear to me that satan knows the children of God, regardless of whether their condition is weak or strong. Do not be surprised when the climate changes at your workplace when you arrive or when you walk into a room. You are a weather changer! Believe me, you do not have to say or do anything for the atmosphere to change rapidly about you, or for a storm to blow up. All it takes is your presence for hell to become enraged.

I remember, one evening after church service, feeling slightly hungry. I had planned to give a sister from the church a lift home, but she was hungry too, so we decided to stop at a fried-chicken restaurant across town. We joined a small line on entering the shop and were waiting to be served, when all of a sudden I felt a cold breeze rush past me. I knew that a presence of evil had entered the shop and was somewhere behind us; the presence was really strong and threatening.

All at once, two men forcefully pushed past the people in the line and began talking very loudly and rudely to the young man who was serving at the counter. My church sister and I had already been given our drinks but were still waiting for the rest of our order. As we stood at the counter, one of the men bent over my sister's drink and asked if he could have a sip. When she told him, "No," he immediately flew into an intense rage, shouting, swearing, and threatening to kill us. The people in the line backed away, leaving us standing there to deal with him alone, but we were by no means alone!

Suddenly, he pulled up his sleeves and showed us scars all the way up his arms, shouting that he had killed many people before, so it would not be a problem for him to kill us! How little he knew!

Turning to my sister I said, "It's the devil: don't respond!" At no time was I troubled or ruffled by the situation, for I knew God was in control. Satan was just kicking up a storm because we were on his turf. He was acting through this man, just as he had acted through Herod, Haman, and King Saul.

The man began to call us *dogs*, saying that he knew who we were, but that as far as he was concerned we were still *dogs*. Pacing about the shop as though insane, the man raged on, so much so that even his friend started trying to calm him down, to no avail.

Then he suddenly began laughing violently, shouting that he was going to his car to get his gun to shoot us. As he left the shop, I whispered to God, "Lock him in that car, Lord...lock him in the car!" He stormed out to his car, which was parked directly outside the shop, flung its door open, got in and began rummaging in the glove compartment. Then, all at once he shut the door and just sat there, as though restrained in his seat. All eyes were on him, but he did not move—he *could not* move!

It was amazing! It was as though someone had arrested

him as he got into his car! He was totally subdued! Do you know something? He never returned to the shop! He just sat in that car and never made another sound. I testify that our God put him under car arrest! The Bible declares that, "No weapon that is formed against thee shall prosper; and every tongue that shall rise against thee in judgment thou shalt condemn. This is the heritage of the servants of the LORD, and their righteousness is of me saith, the LORD" (Isa. 54:17).

So, look for the calm, but do not be taken by surprise, or become frightened or discouraged by a storm in its stead. Why? Because you are a weather-changer!

CHAPTER 9

APPROVED

I T NEVER OCCURRED to me that the storm I had awak-
ened to that fateful morning was a purposeful storm.
It never occurred to me that it had arrived because of
God's words of approval, not his disapproval. It is so easy
to think that every storm that blows into our lives comes
because we have done something bad or because we have
displeased God in some way. It is often hard for us to conceive that it could be to do with God's *favor*.

The Gospels paint a vivid picture of Jesus' baptism,
noting how as John plunged Him into the watery depths,
the heavens opened and a dove descended onto His head,
accompanied by a loud voice saying, "This is my beloved
Son, in whom I am well pleased" (Matt. 3:17).

There is something so amazing and exciting about this pas-
sage of Scripture that it warrants our particular attention and
is worthy of our rejoicing. Note *when* the voice of approval
came: *before* Jesus entered the wilderness of temptation; *before*

He had conquered satan; *before* He had performed a single miracle; *before* He had lifted a finger in public ministry. *Before* He had done all this, God made a public declaration of how beloved He was and how pleased He was with Him.

Now, hold on one moment: pleased with Him? Beloved Son? But Jesus had not done anything as yet to prove Himself, so how could God be pleased with Him? How could God the Father call Jesus his Beloved? Because God endorsed Him before He used Him, that is how! Doesn't that excite you? God did not wait until Jesus got to the end of his forty days and nights' wilderness experience before He endorsed Him, neither did He wait until he had conquered the cross, death, and hell: God approved Jesus at the very beginning of Jesus' ministry!

So take this to heart now my friend, God's endorsement of you does not come *after* you have overcome your temptations, your trials, your wilderness experience, or any such thing. It comes a long time beforehand! God approves of you *before*. God is not about to see His children defeated by satan. How can you be defeated when you are approved by God?

Jesus' experience in the wilderness would have meant His certain defeat had He not acquired the approval of God before He entered it! Satan's attacks on you clearly indicate God's approval of you, not His *dis*approval! God would never allow satan to get anywhere near you if you did not have God's approval! You have been approved by God! Do you know what? It happened long before you ever entered your struggles, long before your storms! Now do you see the implications of this? Yes, God's approval says that you can and *will* make it through every trial you are facing!

Often we hear of men and women who go out on a

mission, a mission they say God called them to, but they never accomplish anything! They lose hope, give up on everything, including God, and then become bitter. We are baffled by this and sometimes even use it in our church communities as a harsh example of why we should all stay inside the church's four walls. Filled with fear of the enemy, we think, "If he could do that to them then what might he do to us if we go out? Hey I'm staying put; it's safer here!" That becomes our attitude. We allow ourselves to become chickens, dwelling at ground level, afraid of the big, bad wolf, instead of the eagles we were born to be!

But take comfort from this: if God approves of you, nothing can kill you. Just remember what Jesus said, "Therefore doth my Father love me, because I lay down my life, that I might take it again. No man taketh it from me, but I lay it down of myself. I have power to lay it down, and I have power to take it again. This commandment have I received of my Father" (John 10:17–18). I do not care how long you lie down as though dead, or how much your situation decays or stinks, if you are wearing the approval of the Almighty God, the God who spoke and saw it was done, who commanded and saw it stand fast, then you are getting back up and standing strong! Decay and stench must retreat! The lesson here is not *do not move*, but rather, do not move until you are approved!

It is the approval of God that seals us against everything and anything the enemy of our soul throws at us. It is vital to grasp this. The approval of God equips you to overcome the devices of the devil. It empowers you not only to stand against him, but also to *go* against him and take back what is rightfully yours! Why do you think King David cheated death so many times? He was *approved*!

Approved men and women are like boomerangs: they are often thrown out because of the anointing on their lives, but they keep coming back, much to satan's irritation. Speaking of David, he is a prime example of the depths that a man or woman can sink to, but because of the approval of God on their lives, they rise again!

We waste too much precious time seeking the approval of men, approval that carries no weight where satan's kingdom is concerned. It is the approval of *God* that makes satan and his agents tremble! Believe me, it is God's approved men and women who are going to destroy satan's rule. He cannot stop a man or a woman who has been approved by God! Let me go even further, just so this word can be absorbed into your spirit and so that you can begin rejoicing and praising God for your victory now! For the mere fact that you are in a storm, facing the accusations of the enemy, feeling his fiery darts zooming past your head, facing some of the toughest battles of your life, crying in a lonely valley, rejected and left for dead is all clear indication that you are the Lord's approved, simply because satan only attacks God's approved!

The Bible tells of a man named *Job*. God revealed His approval of this man, and He did not mind sharing it with satan. Yes, when God approves of you, He will show you off! Job went through the most horrendous battles of his life; he was stripped of everything *but* his life, but he could not die either! Why? Because God's approval of him had been uttered by God to satan, "Hast thou considered my servant Job, that there is none like him in the earth, a perfect and upright man, one that feareth God and esheweth evil?" (Job 1:8).

God had endorsed Job, so satan took God's bait and

went after Job, like a bull after a red rag. But, no matter what he threw at Job, he could not get Job to curse God. This was really the making, not the breaking, of Job! Every child of God who has received God's seal of approval must go through a test, *a wilderness experience*, a time of great temptation involving three areas of their lives: lust of the eyes, lust of the flesh, and the pride of life. When you have been approved by God, you will emerge from your wilderness with power, victorious in all these areas. Evidence of God's approval on your life will be as written in Acts 2:22 (emphasis added), "Jesus of Nazareth, a man *approved* of God among you by *miracles* and *wonders* and *signs*." The evidence of your having been approved is the signs and wonders that God will demonstrate through your life when you come out of your wilderness, victorious. You will be amazed at what the Lord will perform through you! If there is one thing of which I am completely certain, it is this: satan should have stopped you before you were approved.

AFTERWARDS WAS WHEN IT BEGAN

Every true believer craves God's approval, to have the heavens opened, to hear His resounding voice uttering His endorsement. What an incredible experience! Yet there will be very few, if any, who will receive it in this way. Nevertheless, it is not the method by which God chooses to deliver His approval that counts, but rather that you have been given it!

One might be forgiven for assuming that, having obtained God's approval, life from there on would be a satan-free zone—all flowery meadows, sandcastles, and sunny skies. I have to say that nothing could be further from the truth!

The reality is a far cry from a satan-free zone! As a

matter of fact, God's approval of you will virtually hand satan a season ticket to your life. In essence, you will become to satan what a pollen-filled flower is to a bumble bee; you will attract his lustful gaze and relentless, determined attention; you will become irresistible to him. He must have you. Make no mistake, God's approval must not be taken as a deterrent against storms, trials, or tribulations. It is better described as a *sealant* for what awaits whoever has been given it. God's approval of you will not initially elevate you, but actually *isolate* you.

Listen, it was *after* God's approval, "This is my beloved son, in whom I am well pleased," that Jesus was driven into the wilderness to meet the full blast of the devil's challenge; His life up until then had been virtually plain sailing. It is *after* God makes an open declaration of you that the real storms will begin in your life. I am not informing you of this in order to make you shudder with fear, but to show you what comes after God approves you. Your confidence must be in the fact that you will come through any and every storm that rages against you, far more powerful than when it began. Why? Because you have been approved!

The Bible clearly shows us that David's storm began *after* God's public endorsement of him through Samuel. Prior to this, he was happily tending his father's sheep. He may have had to fend off the odd lion and bear now and again, but it was all nothing compared with what he encountered *after* his approval. Suddenly, *after* defeating Goliath, he walked right into a fifteen-year storm—a storm that showed itself in the form of Saul, the king of Israel. There was nothing David could do to permanently quell this storm of jealousy, hatred, and murder. He could play a harp every now and then and behave himself wisely, but for the most part, he had to keep moving. David ran for his life like a fox running from the hunt and its bloodhounds.

When did your storm or fight begin? Was it *after* an outward declaration, made by the Lord's servant on your life? Or in that conference you attended—you know, the one where the preacher called you out and spoke a prophetic word on your life? Or *after* your Pastor told you openly what the Lord had shared with him/her regarding you? Flick through the pages of your memory. You will notice that from that moment on, all hell broke loose in your life.

When I began to embrace this word that I am sharing with you for my *own* situation, it became clear to me that God had chosen this trial to fulfill His purpose in me. I call to mind God's declaration of approval on my life, and I can remember when and on what occasions. It all made perfect sense. During a season, which found me struggling with what was happening and why, I came to realize that it was all about God's *approval*, not His disapproval! My storm, at times, seemed as though it would never come to an end! But you know something? It did! That is why I can tell you with complete confidence that yours will pass too!

I do not know how long it has been raging around you, but one morning, in much the same way as I did, you will wake to find that your storm is over! I have no doubt in my mind that if satan had gotten his way, I would have been consumed! But at a time when I was not aware of it, God spoke His approval on my life. All praise to the Most High God; for His word of approval preserves us.

Stand still; and do not allow the devil to fool you into thinking you have failed, or that you are not in God's will. Stand still and allow God's approval of you to catch that old serpent out again, as it has done so many times before!

CHAPTER 10

I WAS ONLY TRYING TO HELP

AN OLD MAN once found a little boy sobbing in a corner with his head bowed. He was clasping something in his hands. The old man asked the little boy why he was crying. The little boy, his eyes awash with tears, replied, "I was only trying to help him."

"Help whom?" the old man replied, puzzled.

"The butterfly! I was only trying to help him get out!"

The little boy opened his hands; and there between his small fingers lay a crumpled, wilted butterfly, lifeless.

"Why did he die?" the little boy asked.

"I saw him in that thing," he said, pointing at the butterfly's cocoon.

"He looked as if he was struggling to get out, so I cut a slit in it, with my penknife. He was happy and flew up into the sky. Then, all of a sudden, he fell to the ground and now he's dead! Why, sir?'"

"Well, it's not your fault," said the old man, putting his arms around the little boy.

"You weren't to know that there was purpose for his struggle. You see, my son, the butterfly needs the struggle in the cocoon, just as you and I need the sunlight to grow. His strength and beauty come out of his struggle in the cocoon, not from his quick release."

We can all learn a lesson from the little boy's story. It is not people's good intentions, or our quest for quick solutions to our life struggles that ultimately achieve God's designated purposes for us. Indeed our haste for comfort will often leave us regretting our intervention.

When God promised Abraham a son, he and his wife, Sarah, were well past childbearing age. (See Genesis 18:10.) It was an impossible promise for anyone but God to accomplish. You see, there is a liberating power and peace that comes from our acceptance of God's ability to bring the impossible to pass. Suffice it to say that whether or not we choose to accept the freedom this truth brings, it does not negate nor deter God's will to perform it. He is not confined to the peripheries of our beliefs, unbeliefs, intellect, or logic.

So God makes this aged couple an impossible promise. Dare Sarah believe it? Dare she put her confidence in it? All her life she had suffered with silent dignity the shame of a barren womb. Yet how she still longed for a child! Season after season she had stood by and watched as other women conceived and gave birth, watched as they carried child after child for their husbands, while all she carried was the scorn and scourge of an unfruitful womb and a husband's disappointment. But now God had told her that she was going to have her lifelong heart's desire, a child! She, Sarah, would have a child!

To dare to believe this must have sent ripples of incredible joy, confusion, and fear to the very core of Sarah's being. Should she laugh? Should she cry? How could this be? To think that now, in her twilight years, she *could* possibly give birth to a child! Oh, just the thought of it! Oh, the joy!

With what must have been intrepid excitement, Sarah looked for the fulfillment of God's promise. But as the months turned to years, Sarah's excitement and belief began to wane as all her waiting yielded no signs of the promise—no morning sickness, no mad cravings, nothing. Each day of the unfulfilled promise left her doubting the validity of God's word.

It had been approximately eleven years since God had first spoken of a child. Sarah was not getting any younger! Her body clock was well past ticking; in fact, its springs had rusted over and its chimes had fallen off! This promise was now not merely impossible, it was hilarious, and in Sarah's view, time was not simply against her, it had actually left the room, locked the door, and thrown away the key! But I hear our God declare in His Word that what He opens, no man shuts, and, regardless of what time was saying, God held the key that would open Sarah's womb.

However, because of Sarah's growing lack of belief in God's ability to bring His word to pass, she concocted what she thought to be an ingenious plan. She came up with a plan of her own to bypass her lifeless womb and still get the child of her dreams. She decided to send her maid, Hagar, to her husband Abraham. This way, he would have his son and heir, and she would have her baby, her dream! As for

God, well, God looked as though He needed the help, right? *Wrong*, very wrong! Hagar and the child she would bear would become Sarah's nightmare, not her dream!

All too often we hear God's promises, but we are unprepared or unwilling to go through the process of achieving those promises. We want to have the one without the other. Sometimes in our attempts to bypass God's process (for every promise He makes, there is a process), we unwittingly interfere in His plan for the promise. We have to accept the process of His promises. You see, they come as a package deal, a full board of promise and process, all-inclusive, not a self-catering package.

Sarah, like many of us, thought she could carry out, or bring to pass, a promise that she had not made. But this was no earthly promise made by a man or a woman. This was designed in heaven, spoken by the Eternal One. It simply was not hers to live up to; it was God's. He was its author and the One who would bring it to pass in His way and His time. Irrespective of how unrealistic His promises might appear, they do not require our intervention to make them happen! God is not intimidated, rushed, or guided by our need to have Him accomplish His word in our time. Neither can He be seduced or manipulated. He will not accept anything other than what He has purposed and promised. Sarah learned His standard the hard way.

Now when Hagar went in to Abraham, she conceived and gave birth to a son, Ishmael. It looked for a while as if Sarah's plan had worked! Perhaps if God were like you or me, He would have accepted Hagar's child, Ishmael, as His child of promise—but He is not like us. When He made that promise to Abraham and Sarah, He made it with the full intention, ability, power, and integrity to keep it with or without Sarah's aid. His promised child was not Ishmael.

I cannot recall in the Scriptures any account of God's taking Sarah to one side to solicit her help. But you know what women can be like sometimes—we "only try to help," whether we are asked to or not. It is our nature! (God did refer to us as "helpmeets," didn't He?) The problem is that like Sarah, we sometimes get slightly confused as to who requires our help. Anyway, by her actions Sarah was sending a very clear message to God that she had written off the possibility of His promise. What she failed to discern was that God's promises have no regard for any situation— whether it is Sarah's womb, age, belief, or unbelief. Yes, it seemed an impossible promise, but not to the One who had spoken it. Sarah's interference produced a child who was later to become a thorn in her flesh. She must daily have regretted her attempt to help God.

Have you ever jumped the gun before? Have you ever done something that seemed to be the right course of action at the time, only to have it backfire on you? Any time we attempt to achieve God's promises through or by our own devices, it will only be a matter of time before it comes back to haunt us, as in the story of Frankenstein's creation, turning into a monster that finally destroyed him! Yes, there are some things that are simply best left to God. Yet in all fairness to Sarah, her intentions, though naive, were good. But in trying to help God to accomplish His aim, Sarah forgot one small detail: He is the Creator and she the creature. Through her lack of belief in God's ability to be a Promise-Keeper, she interfered in the process of the promise, only to create an offence in her own home, (see Gen. 16:5).

How embarrassed and frustrated we can become when

God's promises do not come true *when* we think they should or *how* we think they should. We begin to act as though God, the Ancient of Days, requires our assistance. Rolling up our sleeves, we jump ahead of Him to set things straight for Him. But the God who stretched out the heavens and spoke the world into existence would not be God if He needed our help to keep His promises!

Sarah had run out of patience and needed an *increase* of faith. So what do *you* do when the promise is taking longer to come than your faith can stretch? What do you do when you look for signs of God's promises to you, but find none? What do you do when there is no further need for the promise, because the situation looks so hopeless that not even the promise could resurrect it? Well, I will tell you what you should not do. You should not try to help! Whatever promise God makes, He will make it good!

What is the promise that you have been waiting for? Has it been so long coming that its purpose seems no longer to be necessary? Remember, every promise is made for a specific purpose. So if the purpose you thought the promise related to now appears null and void, then that is exactly what the promise was made for—a null and void purpose, not a living one.

When Lazarus, the brother of Martha and Mary was laid up ill, his sisters sent for Jesus to come and help, but Jesus deliberately delayed His arrival. Now the sisters did not mind waiting for the promise (Jesus) to come, as long as He came before the purpose (Lazarus) died.

But when the purpose (Lazarus) died before the promise (Jesus) arrived, the Bible says that Martha ran out to meet Jesus as He arrived saying, "Lord, if you had been here, my brother would not have died" (John 11:21, NIV).

I Was Only Tryin

Martha's words exhibited her level of faith; she be_ but only so far. She knew, without a shadow of doubt, that her brother would still be alive if Jesus had not arrived late. Her belief in the power of the promise (Jesus) did not stretch to the dead, decomposing purpose (Lazarus).

Martha thought that the promise (Jesus) was coming for the healing of her sick brother; but in fact, the promise (Jesus) was coming for something far greater. God's plans for our lives are always far more exorbitant than we can ever begin to imagine or indeed expect!

While Martha and Mary were thinking, "Let's heal him from his sickness," God was saying "Let's raise him from the dead!" It is true to say that at times we, like Martha and Mary, get our wires crossed about what God really wants to do for us. We think God is going to do something one way, when He really has no intention of doing it that way at all. So when it does not happen our way, we become disillusioned and discouraged.

"Where is God?" we cry from our malignant, dead, or dying situation, and the reply reverberates, "He's still here; hang in there! He is working for you, but maybe not in the way, the time, or for the purpose you had in mind!"

Like the little boy and the butterfly, if we attempt to meddle with God's process, or to accomplish it *for* God, we stand in danger of regretting our actions somewhere along the road. It is always better to wait and attain God's gift *His* way than to end up with something we have manufactured for ourselves.

The temptation from satan is that we attempt to do for ourselves what only God can do, to take the brush from the hands of the great Master Painter to paint a picture we have not seen, known, or have indeed understood. We must resist this temptation and allow the process of God's promise to run its course without our trying to help and getting in His way!

God's promises set into motion a process not unlike the butterfly's cocoon. It is in this tight, lonely darkness that we receive God's divine anointing and beauty. None of this will come from our being quickly released by instant fixes, but by what will, at times, be intense, prolonged, tearful struggles and sufferings.

The memoirs of many great men and women of the Bible and of the present day repeatedly affirm this. We must arm ourselves, then, with patience and forbearance so that the uninterrupted promise-process may proceed, thus allowing the glorious anointing of heaven's insignia to stain our emerging wings.

CHAPTER 11

TALE OF A SEED

SEEDS ARE FOR sowing, and you are that seed.

The nature of the seed is to increase; therefore, given the right environment, the seed sheds its outer coat to reveal its true self. Though buried far beneath the soil, it somehow uses the soil's cold moist clutches to cultivate itself. You see, the seed's real potential can only be realized through its willingness to be sown. Now a seed, in and of itself, appears insignificant, but to be concerned only with its looks is to underestimate the veiled power that dwells within its inconsequential exterior!

How often have we eaten an apple, or any other seeded fruit for that matter, and taken time to observe its seeds? Not often, I suppose, yet the fruit that we so pleasurably consume is the product of an unimportant-looking seed. It is the suffering of that seed that transforms it into its greater self.

You are a seed, and God intends you to increase. There

can be no barrenness in you, for no seed of God's is infertile. You were born with purpose and potential. You have the potential for abundance, but it can only be released through spending a season beneath the manure and soil of life. The apostle Peter speaks of adding to our faith virtue and to our virtue, knowledge; and so he declares a list of attributes that we should possess. (See 2 Peter 1:5.) Then, He goes on to say that if these things are in us and abound they shall keep us from being barren or unfruitful. (See 2 Peter 1:8.)

It is the potential fruitfulness inside you that the enemy wishes to destroy. His aim is always to keep you at surface level, living a superficial life, with superficial faith and vision, operating in shallow love. He will do his best to prevent you from being sown, as an unsown seed is of no use to itself or anyone else.

Jesus Christ allowed Himself to be sown through His painful death on the cross, so that He could yield the abundance He was carrying. It was this abundance that satan wanted to rob Him of when he offered Jesus the kingdoms of this world and their glory. Satan knew that if he could just deceive Jesus into accepting glory outside the suffering and death of the cross, His triumphant life-changing abundance would be locked away from us forever. If the devil can convince you to stay on the topsoil, that is where he will keep you. You see, topsoil believers pose little or no significant threat to his kingdom.

Some months ago, I was in the city center, wandering around the shops, thinking about God, and enjoying the sunshine when I came across a vast building project. The builders were clearing the ground to erect a high-rise shopping plaza. I noticed that they were in the process of demolishing an old derelict building, which had been standing there for many years.

I was amazed by the precision used by the demolition team to bring that old building down. They did not just blast it to smithereens, but they took it down, one stage at a time. In some areas they used demolition cranes, while in others, they used small, controlled explosions.

Weeks later, I returned to the site, only to find no trace of the old building! As I peered over the fence at the place where it used to be, I was absolutely astounded at how far down the builders were digging, just so they could lay the foundations of the new building. The hole was vast and incredibly deep, so deep it almost made my head spin. I am not talking fifty or so feet. I am talking hundreds of feet down!

Moving away, I began to see the similarities between that building project and God's building project—us. God must demolish the former self before erecting the new one. The old self, with its carnal ways has to die—often demolished piece by piece. God, with timely precision, takes us down, in order to build us up again, anew and afresh, in His own glorious image. He does not tear us down without care, clumsily or haphazardly, but in His tender love.

Months later I was to return to the site, and this time I found a tall and outstanding new building. What a transformation! It was definitely an improvement over the old one! As I stood there admiring the craftsmanship and splendor of this new building, I heard a voice within me say, "The higher I take you, the deeper I will send you."

Have you ever looked at a really tall tree and thought about how far down in the soil its roots have gone? The higher that tree climbs, the deeper its roots have to plunge.

Often the route along which God will take us, or the depths to which He will allow us to be submerged, make the valley of dry bones look like a children's tea party. However, if God has chosen you, sit tight, because the fact that you are going down is a sure sign that you are coming back up! Consider Jesus: look where He was sown—into the very depths of suffering and trials. Now take a glimpse of where He rose—to the very seat of power and authority, at the right hand of His Father!

There will be times in your life when it seems that there is no bottom to the place where you are being sown. You might feel as though you are going down into an abyss of nothingness. You suddenly find yourself in a world of deep darkness where your days of sunlight seem to be gone forever. But trust that it is only for a season. That one unsuspecting day the soil of your affliction will part, and you will burst forth into the most glorious light of morning!

It is through the soil of our suffering that we send down strong roots. They hold us in the purposes of God for our lives. How many times have I let go, fallen, given up, but still found myself standing? How many days and nights have I considered myself lame, but yet found my spirit leaping? Be assured that the same God who sowed His Son Christ Jesus into the soil of suffering is the same God who is sowing you in yours. He will not leave your soul in hell, neither will He suffer His holy one (you) to see corruption. In other words, what you are going through will not destroy you because God will not allow it to.

Wherever you are right now, receive this into your spirit. Regardless of your circumstances, no matter how painful, rough, hard, dark, or cold, believe me, it is only for a season! Spring is on its way and you shall rise! I speak this into the ears of your spirit. Child of the living God, you shall rise; it is only a matter of time.

ARE YOU WILLING?

The dream that Joseph had caused him much pain; the call on the lives of the apostles cost them their lives. Jacob's transformation from a trickster to a prince gave him an injury that he carried to his grave. The faith of patriarch Abraham meant his giving up certain family ties, nearly costing him his son, Isaac. There is pain here, but beyond the pain is joy, unspeakable and full of glory!

Living in the power and authority of God is not about neatly packaged messages, Perspex pulpits, Gucci shoes, and Armani suits! It is not about articulate pronunciations of Greek and Hebrew words. It is simply what the Word of God declares, "If we suffer, we shall also reign with him" (2 Tim. 2:12). When Jesus looked for those who would suffer with Him they fled. Despite all their big talking and pledge-making, when the heat was turned on, they could not bring themselves to suffer with Him.

Have you ever cooked spinach? It is not difficult; it just needs a tiny bit of water and heat. But here is the amazing thing about spinach: no matter how much of it you put in a saucepan, its end result is a far cry from its original state, because spinach shrinks when it meets heat. No matter how much you use, it withers down to almost nothing, and yet it is a struggle to find a saucepan large enough to contain it while it is raw! One has to force it down with the lid, and even then, leaves will be pushing themselves out from under the lid—that is, until it meets heat! After all its swelling talk, when introduced to heat, it shows a very different side to its character—a shrinking side. Let us endeavour not to be spinach-like believers!

The Bible says:

> Many will say to me in that day, Lord, Lord, have we not prophesied in thy name? and in thy name have cast out devils? and in thy name done many wonderful works? And then will I profess to them, I never knew you: depart from me, ye that work iniquity.
> —MATTHEW 7:22–23

Why did the Word declare that He did not know them? Because one can operate for God and yet not be in a relationship with Him. One can use His name, which we all know has power, but not have a true relationship with the owner of that name! God wants relationship-sharers, not name-swearers!

God is willing to have a relationship with anyone who is willing to have relationship with Him, regardless of what they call themselves. God wants relationship-seekers, people who want *Him*, not establishments, organizations, movements, or institutions. He wants us to know and love *Him*, not our own ideas of Him.

Paul shows us that there is a fellowship that we have when we identify Him:

> That I may know him, and the power of his resurrection, and the fellowship of his sufferings, being made conformable unto his death.
> —PHILIPPIANS 3:10

We have been likened to clay, and for clay to be molded into the vessel that is in the mind of the potter, God, it must first yield itself to the hand of the potter. There must be no resistance, or the vessel will be spoiled. The molding process is one that will shape us into the image God has in His mind for us. This is a process that requires obedience.

So great must be the desire of the clay to reflect the potter's mind that it yields willingly to His hands. It is on the wheel of submission that God waters us with the wondrous, and fertilizes the womb of our souls with promises—promises so incredible that we dare not utter them even to our closest companions. And there on this same wheel, in that lost harmony once shared by the divine Creator, God, and His creation, man, begins again, in the magical place where divinity and humanity touch, harmonize, and agree begins again the supernatural relationship between created and creator. It is in this simple ingredient, obedience and submission, that man finds again his soul, his life, his God.

CHAPTER 12

SMOKESCREENS AND BOOBY TRAPS

A SMOKESCREEN IS OFTEN used in military action, to conceal the approaching force's activity. Satan uses this same tactic in a cunning ploy to distract us, or take our focus from God and His promises to us. He used the smokescreen on Eve in the Garden of Eden, pretending that he was concerned about her and her husband; He cunningly used it as a disguise to plant a seed of doubt in Eve's mind about God's loyalty to them, using the very words that God had spoken to them. Eve was taken in; she missed what was really happening, and fell into his trap.

While asleep one night, I saw myself being attacked by a group of twisted-looking, demonic spirits. One member of the group, apparently the ringleader, stepped forward and angrily told me to hand over my keys. I was holding my keys in my right hand, and I gripped them even more tightly, because somehow I knew that if I gave them to him he would have complete access to my life: my car, my house, and my workplace—everything!

As he approached me, he pulled a weapon from inside his coat and wheeled at me, saying, "We're going to see what you look like bald." The others began to laugh as they walked behind him in my direction. He grabbed me by my hair and began to plunge his weapon into my head. I remember crying for help, and I could hear the laughter and taunts of the others, "I wonder what she will look like bald!" they shouted, as he tried to cut my hair.

Then grabbing my right hand, he plunged his weapon into it. "Give me your keys!" he demanded.

"No!" I replied, with more determination than before. "I won't give you my keys! If I give you my keys I might as well be dead!"

Continuing his assault on me, pulling and cutting at my hair, he shouted again, "I said, give me your keys! I've already made you a laughing stock! I have taken your husband; I have taken your house; I have taken your job! Now, you have nothing. Next, I'm coming back for your children! You are nothing!"

I remember thinking, "He is going to have to kill me, because I'm not letting go of my keys!" Cringing under the pain and crying, I remember thinking, "If I just had enough strength to get the knife out of his hand..." Then I heard a voice immediately say, "You have the strength." On hearing these words, I grabbed the hand holding the knife and turned it in on him.

Suddenly the laughter of his friends stopped. I will never forget the look on his face, one of complete astonishment! I felt the strength I now had, and it was incredible. Over

116

and over again, I hit out, and with each blow, he became smaller and smaller, until he vanished.

After defeating him, I put my hand to my head and arm, to feel for any wounds or blood. To my amazement, there was nothing! It was as if I had not been attacked! Satan will always try to overcome us in one of three areas, which I would describe as doors, the lust of the eyes and the lust of the flesh, or the pride of life.

Watch Out! There Is a Thief About!

Doors have handles. It is these handles—of anger, hate, gossiping, backbiting, unforgiveness, arrogance, bitterness, and so on that satan seeks to use to gain access into our lives. He is no fool; he is persistent in his endeavor to steal, kill, and destroy. (See John 10:10.) He will sporadically try these handles over and over again, especially at a time when you least expect it, just like a thief looking to break into a house.

It is rare that a thief will break into a house on the spur of the moment. Usually, a good deal of initial research and planning goes into his effort. He will choose the house that he thinks will yield the most profit and which probably contains costly valuables. He is not just going to break into any old house. It has to be worth his while. Some of his research will involve observing the home's comings and goings: when it is occupied, when it is empty; what windows or doors are left open regularly; how long the premises are left empty, whether the property is alarmed, whether it has a guard dog, and so on. The house stands a better chance of avoiding the thief's attentions if it is in good repair and has some form of warning system.

However, though the thief may well have all the above

information, he might not necessarily strike until he has gone around the house checking it, trying to find an area that yields under pressure, an area which shows itself to be a potential way in. Then, when he feels sure of his plan and his route of entrance, he might make his move, perhaps when the house's owner has gone out, or late at night when he presumes everyone to be asleep. One thing is almost certain: his route will be by way of the area that he found to be the weakest.

Not to have the areas of lust of the eyes, the flesh, and the pride of life securely under the lock and key of Jesus Christ's shed blood is to leave oneself vulnerable. It is to allow satan certain victory. This thief, satan, tried all of these doors in the Garden of Eden. He turned and rattled their handles, only to find *all* of them wide open. He did not hesitate to walk right in with his usual intention—to steal, kill, and destroy.

Adam and Eve are not the only ones who have felt the loss and pain of a ransacked, burglarized life. The Bible gives us many accounts of men and women who neglected to heed the danger of giving any opportunity to the thief of all thieves. As a result, they suffered, because of their failure to be alert, conscious, observant, and disciplined. Satan has not really changed his method of attack. Why should he? His smokescreens have maimed, killed, fooled, ensnared, and distracted so many that it would be foolish to change something that obviously works so well. His aims are very simple and consistent: he will attempt, or is already attempting, to pull the same stunt on you, so do not allow yourself to be fooled!

Are you so caught up with defending yourself that you end up displaying mistrust instead of faith and hope? Are

118

you so engrossed with your own suffering that you end up opening the door to self-pity instead of power? Are you becoming so disappointed with what you do not have that you end up failing to recognize the abundance you *do* have? Beware—you could be creating an access in your life for satan to walk in! You can prevent it by being on alert to it!

The apostle Paul tells us in his letter to the Colossians to set our affections on things above, not on things below, because he knew from his own experiences the acute power and strength of heavenly focus. (See Colossians 3.) Only when we allow the focus of our hearts to be on God will the radiant light of His countenance illuminate, expose, mend, and heal every dark crevice of our lives.

Prior to Jesus Christ's birth and victory over death, satan sought to steal from every person who entered this world. He appeared to have the upper hand. But that was only until Jesus got here; after that the tables turned on him. The power and authority that he stole from us in the Garden of Eden and used to enslave us have been given back to us. On Jesus' resurrection day, all of heaven broke loose in hell. Now we, the children of God, have the ability to discern his devices, his traps, and his charades—as long as we stay focused.

Now we so enrage satan that, just as Pharaoh gave the orders for the slaughter of hundreds of Hebrew baby boys, he sends out directives to have *us* destroyed. But the fact is he cannot kill us; he cannot destroy us! He does not have the authority, and he knows this! So he uses devices such as smokescreens and booby traps to incite us to destroy ourselves.

Now it is important to remember that although satan

119

is the father of all lies, as Jesus said, he will actually use elements of reality in his lies. My attack that night clearly demonstrates that the devil will attempt to distort the truth for his destructive ends. He told me I had lost my house when in fact I had not yet lost it. I was simply falling behind in my payments. He said that I had lost my job when the truth was that I had not lost my job, but was having serious problems at work with management. He told me that I would lose my children, but again, the whole truth was that my children were going through bad spells of illness. Do you see how he twisted the truth? He used a smokescreen of half-truths to drive fear, intimidation, and mistrust of God into me. Always remember that satan will always attempt to instill doubts, fears, and guilt in your mind and heart.

Think of a time when you have come under his attack: I can guarantee you that he used a trace of reality in his accusations, mingled with lies. In my vision that night he was trying to frighten me into conceding, into thinking that he had the power to destroy me! When, really, if that were truly the case, why would he have had to ask for my keys? Why didn't he just take them? Think about it: would satan *ask* for anything he has the power to take? Unless, of course, he *hasn't* got the power to take anything we do not give to him!

Therefore, irrespective of how beaten up, weak, cast down, broken, or despondent you are, you still hold a position of authority over him! At any moment when you decide or realize that you are not as weak or powerless as you think you are, and you open your mouth and speak the Word, you will be surprised at just how fast satan will get out of your way. Remember, it was only when the woman with the issue of blood changed her perspective and began to push in the direction of Jesus that the crowds began to part before her.

WHICH MOUNTAIN?

Many of us are deceived into accepting those things that the enemy presents to us, believing them to be from God. However, in saying this I am conscious that we should not become so preoccupied with the enemy's workings that we lose sight of the power and authority we have through our risen Lord, Christ our hope of glory who dwells within us!

Yet I am also aware of the importance of not being ignorant of satan's wiles of which deception and replication are two of the primary examples. He will try to imitate the workings of God in an attempt to steer you away from what God really intends for you. There can be no better illustration of this than the time when Jesus was confronted by satan in the wilderness of temptation. There, everything that God had already purposed for Jesus was replicated with satan's sinister twist of God's words. Just as it is true that all that glitters is not gold, so it is true that not every mountaintop experience is of God. Some might be of satan.

Now there are two very contrasting mountaintop experiences that you will be exposed to in your walk with God: one to which you will be led by God and the other, taken by satan.

I will not forget the mountain *I* was taken to, and told to jump from; it was during my time of great pressure and strain. It appeared that my marriage was falling apart at the seams. All of a sudden our ability to communicate with one another without arguing appeared impossible. I had become totally weak and discouraged through trying. One morning, after a harrowing night of disagreement, I buckled under its intensity and ferocity. As I sank to my knees, desperately weeping, I felt as though I was being taken away, yet somehow not moving from the floor of my living room. Then suddenly I saw myself on the edge of an extremely high precipice, and I could hear a voice from below clearly saying, "Jump, let go, just let yourself fall, you might as well. No one cares about you. Let go, it will be better for you, the pain will stop; you won't have to worry about anything again, just let go, and you will have peace. You will find comfort here, so just jump, let go." Instantly I recognized that this was not God and I began to quote from Psalm 27:2–3:

> When the wicked, even mine enemies and my foes, came upon me to eat up my flesh, they stumbled and fell. Though an host should encamp against me, my heart shall not fear.

I felt myself immediately coming back, to myself. I remember wiping my eyes and getting up from my knees with more determination than ever, shouting into the air, "No way, satan, you're not getting rid of me that easy!"

Do you see the smokescreen? I was in pain, I *did* need comforting, and I *was* looking for a way to ease my troubles. Nonetheless, if I had accepted what was being offered to me, I would have jumped headlong into the depths of insanity. But, thank God, the Bible declares that, "My sheep know my voice and a stranger they will not follow" (John 10:3–4, author's paraphrase).

Remember I told you that satan will always try to replicate what God is doing? Allow me, then, to distinguish between the two mountaintop experiences for you:

- God will always lead you to His mountaintop.

- Satan will take you to his.

- God's mountaintop experience will come at a time when you are on the threshold of a mighty move in your life, a time of an impartation of strength and zeal from Him.

- Satan's mountaintop experience will come at a time when he thinks you are at your most vulnerable, physically or otherwise.

- The mountaintop of God will always motivate you to worship Him.

- The mountaintop of satan will tempt you to worship anything or anyone but God.

- The mountaintop of God will enlighten you.

- The mountaintop of satan will leave you confused.

- The mountaintop of God will encourage the faith, hope, and love in you.

- The mountaintop of satan will seek to sow the unfruitful seeds of unrighteousness in you.

- The mountaintop of God will leave you transformed.

- The mountaintop of satan will seek to disfigure you.

- The mountaintop of God will empower you.

- The mountaintop of satan will seek to have you hand over your power.

- The mountaintop of God will show you abundance of life.

- The mountaintop of satan will call you to take your life.

- The mountaintop of God will lift you up.

- The mountaintop of satan will seek to cast you down.

- The mountaintop of God will leave you shining in His glory.

- The mountaintop of satan will seek to rob you of any glory.

There will always be discrepancies and inconsistencies between what satan tells you God has said and what God has actually said. Remember, he always attempts to parallel or replicate God. Look carefully at those things that present themselves to you. Do they oppose the Word of God? If they do, they are not of God.

Have you ever tried to complete a *spot the difference* exercise? There are two seemingly identical pictures, but one has to look carefully to find the changes in one picture. The differences are there, but easily missed, because they are often so small. Well, satan presents the same counterfeit to the people of God time and time again, and one has to be earnest in spotting the difference between what he pretends and what God has promised.

While the angels were ministering to Jesus in the wilderness during His forty-day fast, it is certain that Jesus felt physically drained and weak. After all, though He was wholly God, He also was wholly man—or human! This was an opportunity not to be missed by satan: he seized it to try to entice Jesus into opposing the will of His Father, by putting Him through a succession of temptations. Though Jesus was physically drained, He was still spiritually alert; and He used the truth and integrity of God's Word against satan.

Every attack of the adversary will come in stages. That is why you hear people who have little or no understanding of spiritual warfare say that trouble always comes in threes, or "when it rains it pours." You see, when the enemy comes against you, he will always have a planned series of assaults. We see this in his attack of Jesus in the wilderness—at base level, first, then he took Jesus to the pinnacle of the temple, and then finally to an exceedingly high mountain.

The first area in which satan will stage his attack is your flesh, the lust of the flesh—your appetites. Now appetite is not necessarily about food, though in the first instance it will probably be just that. Now this might sound like a strong statement, but it is true. If we cannot control the first most basic urge—our appetite that we are all born with, or our drive for food— then it is most unlikely that we will be able to control our appetite for anything else, whether it be sex, fame, money, you name it! Those things are likely, as well, to control us. We must learn how to exercise self-control. We should be in control of our appetites, not vice versa.

This area has to be put under subjection simply because

in order for us to truly depict discipleship, we must first demonstrate godly discipline. In other words, I must be in control of my appetites, not my appetites in control of me. Our appetite for food is one of the first areas of our lives that will be challenged by satan. All human beings have a need for food; the battle for life in the Garden was fought and lost via the stomach, and again fought and this time won in the wilderness of temptation, again initially via the stomach. Note the first temptation that satan came to Jesus with was, "Turn these stones into bread."

Remember it was through Adam's lack of control regarding his stomach that he lost everything: satan didn't have to lift a finger against him. All he used was Adam's own very natural, yet uncontrolled, appetite to destroy him. Man saw; man desired; man took; man ate; and man died. So then it is abundantly clear that our first discipline can only be gained through learning to use the effective tool of fasting.

Because man is not just soul and spirit, but body, it is essential that he eats regularly to stay healthy. It is good and necessary that he fast from time to time to enhance his spiritual growth. When he fasts, he is feeding the soul and spirit, He is giving them preeminence over the body, as it was in the beginning of Creation, before the fall of man—spirit, soul, and body.

Fasting is important because it gives God back the control over our lives. Understand that before Adam fell, in the Garden of Eden, man was spirit, soul, and body, but after the fall satan turned that order around to body, soul, and spirit, forcing us to put ourselves first and God last. Fasting brings back God's original order. It allows us to put God first in our lives by strengthening us spiritually.

Fasting, carried out orderly and sensibly, is one of the most commanding weapons in our arsenal because it enables us to take authority inwardly. That is to say to be in control of ourselves, and once we have restrained the self, we are on our way to conquering anything that the devil can throw at us. If Jesus hadn't had authority over His basic appetite, He would not have conquered in the three areas of lust of the flesh, lust of the eyes, and the pride of life. He had learned how to deny the flesh for the betterment, empowerment, and rule of the Spirit.

Know this: you will never have authority over anything in your life until you first have authority over yourself. Jesus had the wherewithal to declare, "It is written: Man shall not live by bread alone, but by every word that proceedeth out of the mouth of God" (Matt. 4:4). In other words, we do not live to eat, we eat to live. Just as there is a physical need to be fed, there is also a spiritual need.

It is essential that we have our minds girded about with the truth, and what *is* truth? Truth is Jesus Christ Himself. Jesus said, "I am the way, the truth, and the life" (John.14:6). In order for you to recognize and combat the adversary's deceptions, you must have the Lord wrapped around your mind. For only then will the adversary's smokescreens and booby traps be revealed for what they truly are—traps devised to entangle us

BOOBY TRAPS

A booby trap is a harmless-looking device, but it is one that can have terrible consequences. Satan wants us to take hold of his harmless-looking gifts and to have them explode in our faces. Remember Samson? His legacy to us is, "Don't play with satan's booby traps," for, although they may appear harmless, they are far from it.

When I consider this man, I see someone who had not taken authority over his selfish desires. His appetites were way out of control and therefore getting the better of him. Samson allowed his uncontrolled appetites to destroy him. Inward control will lead to an outward show or illustration of the anointing of God on you.

Sometimes we just talk and debate too much, instead of just standing still and allowing God to give us the answers to satan's arguments. If Eve had not gotten into a debate with the serpent, she would not have shown her vulnerability. Satan will draw us into debates, into much talking and questions, just as he did with Eve ("Hath God said?" [Gen. 3:1]), and as he tried with Jesus in the wilderness ("If thou be the Son of God, command…" [Matt. 4:3]). But we have to know when to talk and when to hold our peace. Just as Eve did not know when to hold her peace, so Samson obviously had not learned this either; he talked and played with the enemy far more than was safe, giving Delilah riddle after riddle until he finally divulged the secret of his strength.

What made Jesus so powerful when He stood before His accusers (Pilate, Herod, the chief priest, and the like) was that He would not allow himself to stoop to their level to prove His Lordship through lots of talking; instead He held His peace, while knowing that with just one word from Him, ten thousand angels would have come to His aid. At times, all our irrepressible talking demonstrates just how undisciplined and powerless (instead of powerful) we really are. Satan knows this. We give away secrets we should have kept close to our bosom. It is a strong person who can keep silent in the midst of mockery and contempt.

We have nothing to prove to the devil: he knows our authority already; but his aim is to have you and me use it in disobedience, pridefully. Giving away your purposes, in pride, to satan as a demonstration of your power and authority when he challenges you is bound to lead to aborting the mission to which you were called, and that is his ultimate aim.

There were some at the crucifixion of Jesus who said, "If he be the King of Israel, let him now come down from the cross, and we will believe him" (Matt. 27:42). If raising Lazarus from the dead, giving sight to the blind, feeding the five thousand, and many other miracles He performed had not earned their belief, why should this miracle be any different? It was a booby trap neatly parceled and wrapped, a disguise of the devil to tempt Jesus to use His power in pride and disobedience, thus negating His mission and plunging the world into eternal darkness!

Many great people have lost out because they moved to prove themselves at the adversary's challenge. *Never* move to prove. Know who you are in God and stand your ground. Your approval will speak for you; do not accept the devil's smokescreen or his booby traps. Stay focused on God; stay positioned. It is the adversary's hope that you will destroy yourself in one of the areas I have shown you, as he knows he does not have the authority to do it himself. What a booby trap!

Natural booby traps can be made to look like a gift, a toy, or even food. The sole purpose of the sender is to make it appealing and completely harmless with the intent of taking in the unsuspecting receiver.

Samson learned the hard way about satan's booby traps. He ensnared himself, playing with his God-given gift.

He ruined his own life and the lives of those who were depending on him, because he played with a booby trap. He failed to keep himself under control, and therefore, he had no real awareness of satan's plan for him. He lay down in the lap of the enemy, naively underestimating her cunning. Each time he was with Delilah, she begged him to tell her what the source of his strength was. Samson did not smell a rat; he was too busy feeding his unrestrained greedy appetite.

Do you know that Samson never once allowed God to use him for His glory? It was always about Samson, never about God. He behaved like a fool and paid a cruel price for his folly. If you think the enemy likes you, or is playing with you, read what happened to the mighty Samson. The enemy took his hair, put out his eyes, and turned him into a slave and a laughing stock. Do not play, or even entertain, the adversary's smokescreens and booby traps. They will explode! (See Judges 16:21.)

CHAPTER 13

HE CAN'T MAKE YOU

ALWAYS BE AWARE that even at your weakest point you do not have to hand over anything to the devil. Any authority that he wields over you is what *you* have given to him! He can take nothing from you! You have to hand your authority to him for him to have authority over you! Just as he could not take my keys out of my hands or push Jesus off the edge of the mountain, he does not have authority over any one of us!

Understand that the one who can do you the most harm is not a friend, not an enemy, not satan, but *you*, you and only you; you alone have the authority to speak strength into yourself through all your weaknesses, failures, problems, whatever they might be! You might be surprised to find how much strength you have.

Don't Waste Your Pain

You Are Not Your Circumstances

Many of God's people are bent low under loads of circumstances, believing that they must *be* what is happening to them. But we must believe; we are *not* our circumstances! Though it is important that we learn from our mistakes, so that we do repeat the same mistake again. How we got there, or how it happened is more a matter for you than it is for God. He knows all of that already!

Looking back at the woman with the issue of blood, I realize that Jesus never once said, "Explain why you are so ill," or "How did you get yourself into such a state?" His sole aim was to congratulate the woman on her move of faith. As a matter of fact, at no time during His stay on earth do we read of Him asking any of those He healed how they had got into that particular situation.

Do you know that it brings great pleasure to God to see His children moving towards Him for help? Even though, in most cases, they knowingly walked into the bad situations they found themselves in. He loves us, and He continually wants the very best for us, no matter what we have done or where we have been!

It is not in the nature of God to say, "I told you so," remember it is satan who is the accuser of the saints, not God. God does not need to accuse us of anything! He cannot lie. He does not stand there wagging His finger and shaking His head when we fail or when we are weak from the trials of life. His love for us is everlasting; He means us no ill; His thoughts for us are for good and not evil. When we suffer, He is not some sadistic deity, taking pleasure out of our pain. Being with us, He feels it too.

When Jesus hung on the cross, bearing the wrongs all of

mankind, did God love Him any less because of where He was, in a position of shame and disgrace? Remember that death on a cross was a shameful death. To die on a tree was seen to be a very dishonorable way to die. No! He loved Him with the same intensity, with the same force!

Perhaps you have failed in life and you are in a place of shame right now. Perhaps you did something you ought not to have done and have brought shame and embarrassment on yourself and your family; perhaps you were in a place of esteem and renown, but because of your sin you have been humiliated, exposed, degraded, and stripped of your position. I say to you now that Jesus bore your shame. He bore your disgrace! Yes, you might have done the things you have been accused of; but you are not damned. Get up from where you are. You are going to come back a better person for what you have been through! You may be in a *place* of disgrace, but *you* are not a disgrace! Folk may have labeled, scorned, entombed, and buried you, but I am sure of something: if you repent and humble yourself through it all, I dare anyone to keep you down!

Sometimes I get the impression that we feel that repenting of some wrongdoing or some failure means winning back God's love for us again. But how can we win back something we never lost in the first place? He has never *stopped* loving us. It is not a case of God merely loving. God is love! His love for us is undying, never-ending, and unconditional, no matter where we have been or what we have done, or how our actions have left us feeling about ourselves or others feeling about us. Believe me when I say that God loves you, *regardless.*

You are not your circumstances, you are not the failure, and you are not the sin! I often hear folk say, "I am such a mess!" but *I* say, "Don't own the *situation* as being you!" I say, "The situation you find yourself in might be a mess; but that doesn't make *you* a mess. That's exactly what the devil wants you to believe. He wants you to believe that you are that failing marriage, that you are that illness, that you will never amount to anything."

But right now, by the power of the blood shed by the Savior at Calvary, I declare to you that you are *not* that situation! Wherever you are at this point in your life, *push through the pain* of disillusionment and discouragement, *push through the pain* of loneliness, depression, failings, and sin. Don't own it! Push through it!

Let God be God. We struggle unnecessarily in trying to get into people's good books, hoping to be noticed or wanting folk to like us, believing that perhaps in their presence or having their favor will make our lives better in some way. But I have come to realize that it is not the favor of man that we should crave. For people will love you today and hate you tomorrow. The ones who lined the streets and cried "Hosanna" for Jesus were the same ones who, one week later, cried, "Crucify Him!"

The only good book that you or I should be interested in (apart from the Bible, of course!) is that final one, the one that revelation speaks of: *the Lamb's Book of Life.* Now that is the one book that, at the end of your days when all is said and done, will count for anything and everything. The only favor that counts for anything is that of God, for when we have *His* favor, everyone and everything else will fall in line in His plans of favor for us. Even when folks don't like you, the Bible says that they have to be at peace with you. (See Proverbs 16:7.)

Long before you got here God knew you and made

provision for you. There is nothing about your life that can take God by surprise! You will not find God saying, "I didn't know she'd do that!" or "Well, what do you know?" When God speaks, there are words and phrases in our vocabulary that are quite frankly not in His, such as:

Maybe

Might

Perhaps

Hum? (Can you imagine God saying *hum*? I don't think so!)

Pardon?

Oh, you surprised me!

I didn't mean what I said...

Do you think that it was easy for Jesus to come up out of the grave just because He was Jesus? No, it was hard! Every day He found something new grabbing hold of Him and trying to keep Him down—like some new accusation, some lie, some guilt, some act of unforgiveness, some wound, or pain. He had stuff grabbing at Him and pulling Him down further and further into the pit, but He refused to stay down, refused to allow them to stop Him from getting up.

When God, through this book, or through the mouth of the preacher, teacher, or prophet tells you that, "You are not your sin; you are forgiven; you are not your circumstances," no matter how bad you feel or how you are being made to feel, God wants you to know that you are not what is happening to you, so believe it! Get up, brush yourself off, and move on! You can do it! You can rise up out of this—this thing that threatens to hold you down for the rest of your life! You *can* rise above it, so come on, *PUSH!*

GOD KNOWS

While I was in prayer concerning this chapter, the Lord gave me these words for you.

> I know the weight of your loss, the overwhelming force of your grief. I know and have seen your hurt, how sad you have been when you looked for hope in the eyes of your loved ones and found hopelessness and apathy. I know and have seen your anguish in looking for answers to issues that have no rhyme or reason. I have seen you living within arms' reach of so many people, yet feeling so afraid and so alone. I know that you feel as if you've cried for so long, you can't remember how to laugh. I know that you are just going through the motions of living, but that inside you surely feel as though you are dying. I know how afraid you are of lying down, for fear you'll never get back up again. But I will cause your bleeding to cease.

The words "I know" spoken by God must not be taken lightly, or equal to our use of it. By comparison, our knowledge even at best, when we are certain, is so limited.

We find that, despite all we know, there is still so much that we have to admit that we do *not* know. But this cannot be said of God! Is there anything that God does not know? He knows all things. His knowingness does not merely speak of His knowledge of past, present, and future, nor does it just speak of His intelligence or wisdom. It ascribes Him, *God*! It encompasses His infinity, His authority, superiority, and supernatural power, His authority and power to change things, or indeed *not* to.

Take comfort from the fact that God has said He knows, for indeed what He is saying is "I am in control; it is all right!" God—not me, not anyone—but God has said, "I know." *To you*. Now, that is powerful!

What Does God See?

Michelangelo once said that when he looked at the stone he was about to sculpt, he saw individuals inside the stone, waiting for him to release them. He never saw just a piece of stone, but always the image in the stone; He saw his creation before he hewed it out; He saw it even though no one else could see it.

He knew when to use the chisel and when to use the hammer. Within his hands lay the power to turn stone into the beauty we marvel at today. If all this came from the mind of a mere mortal, then how much more must come from God?

Michelangelo took seven years to paint the ceiling at the Vatican in Rome; during that time those who had commissioned him were losing patience with him—they wanted him to finish it, sooner rather than later. But amidst the cries of criticism and the arguments, he would settle for no less than what he could see.

His critics could not see what he saw; they did not know what patience and what a labor of love it would take to execute a painting of such magnitude, but Michelangelo did. Why? Because he could *see* it: He saw the rainbow of colors; he saw each intricate line, every expression; he saw it all, and so it is with God. He sees *all* things; He knows *all* things. He is painting the most glorious picture through your life as He has done with so many lives before Him. Trust Him when He tells you that He knows, for it speaks of so much more than you can ever imagine!

With His palette poised and with every dash of color, whether dark or bright, with each scrape of the knife and every rub of the painter's cloth, a wondrous, glorious work of art is unfolding within you. His heavenly gallery has housed the framed lives of so many willing men and women who have trusted His knowledge and yielded themselves to His hands. What magnificence these yielded souls have brought to our lives!

God's knowingness speaks of who He is, *Alpha* and *Omega*. His is not a knowledge that has been gleaned from books or past experiences, failings or mistakes. No—His knowingness speaks of His omniscience, deity, supreme sovereignty, power, and authority.

None of us knows the picture God desires to paint with our lives, the colors He will use, or how long it will take to be completed. But be assured of this: as this Master Painter applies His brush to your life, not one stroke will be out of place or without reason. There will be no mistakes, neatly and professionally covered up, neither will there be one color, dark or light, that should not be there. You are His work of art; you will show forth His excellence. Your life, the image it reflects, will indeed furnish Him with the honor and glory He so justly deserves.

Today, historians and artists alike study the works of this man, Michelangelo, and marvel over them. Though they never met or knew the man in person, they have learned so much about who He was, just through the images He left behind. God wants you to act in just that way for Him.

God, in informing you that He knows, seeks to bring you to an understanding of how He works. So often we feel that God could not know what we are going through, or else He would get us out of it. God also seeks to bring peace and rest to your troubled mind and spirit, the assurance that though you are in the midst of your storm, all is yet well! Why? Because God has said that He knows.

We refer to Him as *Deliverer* (and so He is), so we routinely expect that He will of course deliver us from bad things. Right? Wrong! For, so often, what we think we need delivering from, God is taking us through. Often the way God will deliver us from evil is by taking us through its midst. Yes, indeed, He is our deliverer from evil; but His ways are not a boxed in formula.

David wrote in the psalms, "Yea, though I walk through the valley of the shadow of death, I will fear no evil: for thou art with me" (Ps. 23:4). God will not take you out before He takes you through! It is simply not how He works. But the great thing about it is, as David declared, that you do not need to be afraid of the evil because God is right there with you, bringing you *through* it!

The ark that Noah built had to go *through* the flood; the children of Israel had to go *through* the Red Sea and *through* the wilderness; the three Hebrew boys had to go *through* the fiery furnace. We must allow our knowledge of God's knowledge of our situation to reinforce our confidence and trust. God needs no reminder as to *where* we are, or what we are going *through*; He knows. He is the one who has allowed us to be there, and though we cry to be moved, unless it is the right time, we are in fact praying amiss. We must trust that He is bringing us *through*!

Follow me: a baker desires to make a cake, so after blending in all the necessary ingredients, he places the cake in a preheated oven for a given time. Now if the baker removes the cake before the set time, it will be ruined; closed-in heat helps the cake to rise and to open the door on it before that given time will prevent it from rising. The cake must be baked in constant, intense heat to achieve the purpose for which it was mixed.

It was in the fiery furnace of affliction that the Hebrew boys arose to the occasion. It was in the torrential rains that Noah's ark rose to the heights of Ararat. God's route of deliverance very rarely resembles or accords with our idea of deliverance; so often, things might even appear bleaker *after* God has told you that He knows or that He will act than before He said it.

How must David have felt when as the anointed next king of Israel he was hunted and tracked like a fox across the countryside by Saul? Or Job, how must he have felt when he looked at his life, with his body and his family in complete ruin, after satan's vicious attack on him? But both men held their ground, stayed in the heat, and bent with the blows to bounce back, delivered from the evil attacks they walked through. Look at the finished product of these two men—as victors, far more glorious than they were before their trials and afflictions began.

Perhaps as in the fairy tale, *Cinderella*, you have so far warranted no one's attention, no one's time, and most of all, no one's love. But, do you know something? The night of the ball is coming, and unveiling day is fast approaching.

When Cinderella got to her ball that night, all eyes were fixed on her because she was so beautiful. Yes, I know it is a fairy tale, but it is one with a message, so listen! I believe that God is bringing about a transformation in your life even as you read.

Who was this mysterious, beautiful princess who was winning the heart of the prince? Not even her sisters recognized her. This was the girl who had slaved in their home, and had washed and cleaned their clothes. They never saw her as anybody; she was nothing but a scraggy, ragged maid. But this maid had a dream. She had a vision of marrying a prince. You see, I believe that Cinders was never really a ragged, orphaned nobody; she was a cloaked princess, and the ball and the events thereafter were her unveiling day.

Let me assure you that when God gets through doing what He is currently doing with you, it will be all glory. Cinders? That was a fairy tale, but *you*? This is for real!

CHAPTER 14

THE STILL BEFORE HIS WILL

WHEN GOD HAS made the declaration that He knows your situation, He will then follow it with an "I will." This is God informing you what He is going to do about your condition.

God said to the children of Israel, "I will bring you up out of the affliction of Egypt." (Exod. 3:17). Moses and Israel did indeed experience God's will!

There is no doubt in my mind that when God says, "I will," He most certainly will. I find that we are often excited about His declaration (and rightly so), but not prepared for what I call the *still* before His *will.*

Now the still is a crucial period in the life of every believer; it often precedes God's promises of blessing, healing, and deliverance, and therefore, it is essential that we comprehend it and are prepared for it. But what *is* the still?

143

Well, the still is a period of apparent non-activity, a time that God wills after making a promise. It is a season when God may go completely silent, or when He is not doing what you had expected Him to for that situation to change improve, come to pass, or move.

For example, when God told Abram to move and that He would bless him and make his name great, and that out of him all the nations of the world would be blessed, Abram did as he was told, but then all of a sudden God went silent on him. God did not speak to him again on this subject for which he moved in the first place for another eleven years! But that did not mean that the promise God had made to Abram had become null and void because of God's silence, or should I say, His *still*.

The same thing happened to Moses: Moses expected God to just whisk Israel out of Egypt the moment he opened his mouth, but instead God delayed in swiftly delivering them, and the situation began to get very bad. But again, His *still* did not invalidate His promise of deliverance. Once we begin to understand that God's *still* is not an indication that God has changed His mind or deserted us, we can avoid the pitfall of wallowing in the miserable assumption that we misinterpreted, misunderstood, or frankly did not really hear His words.

When Jesus told the disciples that He was going to be crucified, He also told them that He would be raised from the dead on the third day. Now when Jesus was actually crucified, the disciples fainted, they disbanded, and fled. The disciples were not prepared for this. They believed that it was all over. Jesus' body was laid in Joseph of Arimathea's tomb, and then came the *still* before the *will*.

Frequently we faint or fade away before the accomplishment of His will, leaving our positions, as the disciples did, discouraged and disheartened by what we believe to be a failed promise, failing to understand that God had not yet completed His Word and that the Word has to fulfill certain stages before its accomplishment. For His Word will never return to Him void, but it shall accomplish. (See Isaiah 55:11.)

We swallow satan's lies that the worsening of our situations is a certain indication that God has not and *will* not carry out His Word. Now, all of a sudden, we begin to falter and no longer speak with such strength and conviction. We utter words like *maybe* and *might be*. Our conversation degenerates into faithless talk, and we can be heard saying things like, "Okay, my sister, maybe the Lord might just heal you," or, "It might not be the will of God," or, "Oh, I don't really know any more—maybe God is not going to deliver us!"

That old serpent, satan, is having a field day with us simply because we are not fully prepared for God's *still*. If you have moved from your place, discouraged and dismissive of a promise God has given you because it has not happened yet, I tell you now to go back straight away! It is just the *still*! The will is bound to follow!

The Bible tells of the apostle Paul's journey to Rome, and says:

> And when neither sun nor stars in many days appeared, and no small tempest lay on *us*, all hope that we should be saved was then taken away....Then fearing lest we should have fallen upon rocks, they cast four anchors out of the stern, and wished for the day.
>
> —ACTS 27:20, 29

145

Paul's ship sailed straight into contrary winds. How could it? Didn't God know that Paul was aboard? Wasn't he to be a witness for God in Rome? How could Paul's ship encounter a storm? Wasn't there a call on his life? Well, despite all things, Paul's ship did indeed meet a storm. You see, satan wanted Paul dead. Remember the storm of purpose and the storm of abortion of which I spoke earlier? This storm was the one of abortion—where the devil wanted Paul to abort his mission. What better time to have Paul destroyed than right there on board that ship!

The violent storm continued for days, as the ship drifted, with no one able to see the sky because of the darkness of the storm. Just because God has made promises of deliverance to you does not mean that you are immediately going to be able to see the blue skies. Paul held his position; he knew his purpose had to be fulfilled because he was carrying a *word* that had to be delivered in Rome. He could not die with it still inside him, unaccomplished!

Sometimes during the *still* it will appear as though your last glimmer of hope has gone, but hold your position! Stay on board the ship! Drop your anchor and wait, and keep the ears of your spirit open and listen for God. Do not be afraid of being afraid, even when what you are experiencing warrants it, but understand that it is merely the *still* before His will!

The Book of Acts tells us that although Paul received a message from God concerning their safety, things did not automatically get better, leaving some of the crew contemplating abandoning ship. Paul told the centurion who was guarding him and other prisoners that, "Except these abide in the ship, ye cannot be saved" (Acts 27:31). You will be tempted to believe that God will not do what He said He would during the *still*, but do not allow time to be the deciding factor in whether you desert His word or stay faithful. Remember, if He promised it in His Word, He shall bring it to pass!

And remember this also: it was fifteen years from the time David was anointed king to the time he actually sat on the throne. It was eighteen years from the time Jesus showed Himself to be like no other child to the time He appeared in the public arena. It was forty years from the time Moses realized his calling to the time he was actually commissioned and sent. It was twelve years that the woman with the issue of blood suffered at the hands of many physicians before she touched Jesus, and it was three days and three nights that Jesus lay in the clutches of the grave before we saw Him spring forth.

Sometimes we lose faith in God because we feel that His "I will" will never come to pass. But you need to know that when God speaks, His Word comes with clout! This means it comes with influence, power, pull, authority, weight, and effectiveness, so just be still! God has everything under control!

Believe me when I tell you, an "I will" spoken by God on your life must come to pass! No hell, high water, valleys, caves, depression, oppression, sickness, war, famine, pestilence—nothing—can stop it! You can take God at His Word, because He is not a man that He should lie! (See Numbers 23:19.) He is God!

Don't Waste Your Pain

God Will Sing You a Lullaby

> Yet the LORD will command his lovingkindness in the daytime, and in the night his song shall be with me.
> —PSALM 42:8

The definition of a lullaby, from the Oxford Dictionary, is "a soothing song, to send a child to sleep."[1] The Bible declares that we have entered into His rest (Heb. 4:3), but there are situations that arise in our lives which cause us to be restless, wounded, scared, or frightened, and no longer resting in Him. Situations may cause us to become fretful; but God has a lullaby especially composed for His hurting, bleeding children. I know because He sang one to me. You see, I understand what it feels like to go to bed hurting and wake up still hurting; I know what it feels like to look for some sense or answer to your pain and not be able to find one; I know the pain of failure, rejection, loneliness, and fear, and what is more, I know how it feels to hope for the morning only to wake to yet another night.

On the night of September 25, 2000, I went to bed, curled up in a fetal position, afraid, alone, sad, and cast down, and God spoke to me, and then He sang me a lullaby that wiped away the tears of my heart, comforted my soul, and drove away all my fear. It can be hard to understand that good can come from an ache that feels so bad. Mine was a marriage made in heaven that was going through hell. Yes, I had said the vows, for richer and for poorer, in sickness and in health, for better and for worse, and I meant every word of it, but who could

[1] *Oxford Compact English Dictionary* (Oxford: Oxford University Press, 1996).

148

have known that our poorer was going to become so very poor, and just how sick sickness was going to get, or how worse the worse was really going to be.

For the first four years of our marriage things were wonderful, it could not have been better; it was everything I expected and more. But then a storm hit us in the fifth year, a storm that lasted for seven years, a storm so violent that it was all we could do to just hold on. No amount of praying and fasting appeared to lessen its blast, no amount of weeping or beseeching changed its course.

We lost our home in a repossession order, I suffered a miscarriage, and then lost my health to a mysterious illness that rendered me helpless to its onslaught of brutal attacks. My husband lost his job, while I was on the brink of losing mine. And then to make matters worse both of us lost the joy of communicating lovingly with each other as husband and wife and as friends, which more than anything bore heavier than everything else we were going through.

Friends whom I had held dear walked away from us, church support was withdrawn when we needed it the most, and there were times when I felt as though I was losing my mind. We were left with God, our children, our extended family, and our marriage. Even though it felt at times as though it was hanging together by a thread, God was to prove that it was bound together by something so much more stronger than just a thread!

That night of the 25th I retreated to my parent's home. I needed to get away to hide, to make it all go away, and to grieve. Surely God had left us; it was all too hard and too painful to carry anymore. As I lay curled up in bed like a child in a deep sleep, I longed for the morning to come, but dreaded what it would bring; I hoped for the breaking of the day, but felt too broken to rejoice should it appear. The Lord sung me a song and spoke to me.

He told me to comfort His people; He said that He could hear so many of them crying. They were wounded and broken, bleeding and dying, and He wanted them to be comforted. He showed me so many of their hurts and allowed me to hear and feel their sorrow. As I cried, He told me He was going to use me as a balm for the hurts of His people. He continued to speak to me of my own experiences—why I had felt such pain in my own life—then He showed me Isaiah 40, and said, "Bev, I will use you as a balm for My people. I am going to place you in the midst of the hurting, the broken, the grieving, the lost, and the lonely; touch them for Me, even as I have touched you."

While I wept, I felt myself being lifted and gently rocked to and fro. There was such an incredible, overwhelming presence of love, peace, and warmth all around me, actually engulfing me! Then I heard the most beautiful voice singing a truly wonderful song, a song that will stay with me eternally.

I knew that the song had come straight from God's throne room. It struck a chord in me! I felt so safe! It was like no melody I had ever heard before. Yet, it felt familiar. Then, I understood: it was a song sung by a mother, a lullaby sung in the middle of the night to her frightened child, sung as she looked deep into his frightened eyes with her arms firmly wrapped about his small frame. Rocking him gently to and fro, brushing his hair back, wiping the droplets of sweat from his brow and his salty tears from his already stained cheeks—all the time she whispered, "It's all right, you're safe. I am here. I've got you. I love you. I love you." Tenderly squeezing him close to her breast, her lullaby begins; the warmth of her breath caresses his face. As she sings to him, he is safe, he is loved, and he has nothing to fear, for he is in his mother's arms!

When I awoke, my pillow was wet with the tears I had been crying throughout my visitation, and I realized that God, like a mother comforting her frightened child, had sung to me a lullaby. He had held me in his arms, and He had caressed and rocked my fears, hurts, and worries away.

My friend, God will soothe and lullaby all *your* fears and tears away too. He will heal your hurt and cause your bleeding to cease, so that you will laugh again, you will love again, you will be whole again. His lullaby testifies to it. (See Isaiah 40:1– 4.)

CHAPTER 15

SWEETENED TO HER TASTE

Some of my earliest recollections are of my mother making us recite the Sunday school lesson every Saturday evening, without fail. There was a set routine that we all soon became familiar with: polish our shoes, go to her room to pick up the church outfits she had already pressed and laid out neatly on her bed, and then recite our Sunday school lesson until we knew it by heart.

It was many a Sunday morning that my brothers and I would feign sickness so as not to go to church. We were never as tired as on a Sunday morning. My mother would say, "You're never tired on any other day, but on a church day!" And this was indeed true. For Sunday morning was the hardest day of the week in which to get up!

There was never a believable excuse that we could give her, to get us off the hook. But as children we tried every trick in the book. Somehow my mother had this strange ability to know when we were faking it, but it did not stop us from trying!

"Come on, everyone!" she would call from downstairs. "It's Sunday morning, and that means church!" We would roll over, pretending not to hear, and pray that this would be the one morning that she would let us have a lie-in. But "lie-ins" were definitely not a part of my mother's vocabulary when it came to church! Then we would suddenly hear a sterner voice bursting into our bedrooms with a lot more force than before. "It's church! Don't make me have to call you all again!" It was no use. We knew it—we would just have to concede. Oh, how I disliked getting up on Sunday morning!

The aroma of fried eggs and the sound of crackling bacon would waft gently into our bedrooms along with the voice of my mother singing "Guide Me, O Thou Great Jehovah." The clattering of the cutlery as she laid the table for breakfast told us, "Come, for all things are ready!" The house felt warm, calm, and safe. Outside I could hear the church bells ringing over and over and over again as though they too were telling us to "Get up, it's time for church!"

We would never leave for church without a hearty breakfast of sausages, bacon and eggs, and a hot cup of tea, which my mother sweetened to her taste. We never complained, even though there were times when we would try the tea and want more sugar, and other times, when it tasted so sweet that we could hardly drink it. We accepted what she gave us; we just drank. Oh, for the spirit of a child!

Each of us would sit at that breakfast table, immersed in the atmosphere of a God, brought in by this godly woman, our mother. This woman was incredible; she was stern, yet gentle, strong yet loving, peaceful yet insistent. We would eat, drink, and leave the table to get dressed for church. Looking back, I realized that God, just as my mother did for my brothers and me, sweetens our lives to His taste, not asking how sweet we wish it to be, not guided or deterred by our groans of distaste.

Certainly, there have been periods in my life when most of what was on God's menu for me was in no way sweet to me. I cannot count the days and nights that I spent asking God to change the taste: add something sweet or take away something bland, boring, or bitter! But do you know what? He would continue to sweeten to His taste. God said to Isaiah:

> Woe unto him that striveth with his Maker! Let the potsherd strive with the potsherds of the earth. Shall the clay say to him that fashioneth it, What makest thou? or thy work, He hath no hands?
> —Isaiah 45:9

Then there would be times when things seem too sweet to be true, so sweet that I could hardly take it in! David said that God prepares a table before us, but if you read the text, it does not tell us what is on the table! It does not say that it is all sweet. (See Psalm 23:5.) When we read this scripture, we often become all excited as we anticipate the table holding lots of sweet delicious delicacies, believing that it heralds a time when we will finally be able to rejoice before our enemies, a time of great pride, rejoicing, and bliss. But, as my mother once preached, "Not so." This may be true, but only partly. As I have learned, this table does indeed hold sweet and wonderful moments of sheer chocolate and vanilla delight, but it may also hold sour and downright bitter tastes—like sorrow, pain, and suffering—that call for you to experience forgiveness and healing.

Every joy that Jesus experienced while on earth was always in the shadow of the cross. There are always two sides to every coin: where there is bitter, there will always be sweet; where there is joy, there will also be sorrow; where there is high, there will also be low.

Think about it for a second or two: who, in their right mind, would only put all sweet items of food on a table?

One evening after a hard day at work, you decide to go out for a meal. You arrive at the restaurant and are handed a menu and shown to your table. Once seated you run your eyes over the menu and are surprised at what you see; maybe there has been a misprint, you think.

"Waiter!"

He approaches, pen and pad poised to take your order.

"There appears to be a misprint on your menu," you smilingly inform him.

"Could I have another one, please?"

"Misprint?" he replies. Looking rather puzzled, he reaches to take the menu from you, before briefly scanning it and handing it back to you.

"No, madam, I fear you are mistaken; there are no misprints in this menu."

"Are you trying to tell me that the starter is…"

"Pudding!" The waiter answers, before you are able to end your sentence.

"But you've also got…"

"Pudding," he answers again for you.

"For the *main* course?"

"Right, so can I also assume the dessert to be…?"

You pause for him to end your sentence again.

"Pudding!" he answers, with a smile.

"Would you like to order now, madam?"

Now really, would you dine at this restaurant? You wouldn't, would you? Or maybe *some* of you would (smile)! Do you see? We expect from God what in fairness we would not expect from anywhere else. But be assured, my friend, that with every mouthful, every sup, whether bitter or sweet to our taste, God has specially prepared it in His very own kitchen. If it were you or I preparing the table or the meal, we would be sure to furnish it with only the things palatable to our taste. In this case, God is the one doing the preparing, the cooking, the sweetening, and the furnishing of our tables, and we are cordially invited to give thanks and eat.

So sit at this table that He has prepared for you; trust this master chef. He has prepared meals for many before you and will continue to do so long after you have left the scene. Trust that as well as being your Father, He is also your mother; and all that He prepares for you might not always be to your taste. But believe that as the Word of God proclaims, it is working for your good!

His Lessons

Often if we pause for a moment, we can draw deep spiritual truths from the natural everyday occurrences of life. How often I have heard God speak to me more forcefully through life's simple experiences than from a sermon preached from the pulpit. How wonderful it is to think that we can hear God speak at any time we decide to listen. One does not have to be a great Bible scholar or a seasoned believer to hear God. One just has to possess the humility to listen for and recognize His voice. His lessons can be seen in the clouds, the trees, each blade of grass, the cry of a newborn, the bleating of the sheep, the colors of the rainbow, the laughter of a child. His lessons are all around us.

THE PROMISE IN REALITY

My daughter's face lit up at the prospect of going swimming. I had made a promise to her weeks before, and as she had never been swimming before, she was anxiously anticipating the fulfillment of my promise.

Finally the big day came, but as we arrived at the baths, I watched her mood change from excitement to anxiety, then from anxiety to outright fear! As she gazed at the size and depth of the pool, suddenly the promise did not look so wonderful after all. She forgot that I was with her; instead, she was overcome by fear.

As we got closer and closer to the pool, I could feel her grip becoming tighter and sense a hint of reluctance in her once bouncy step. I began to lower her into the water, and she began to scream. She was creating quite a scene. "No mummy, no!" she cried, clinging to me, my reassurances falling on deaf ears. "Just put your feet down and stop struggling," I said. "No!" she cried, then went on to scream at me that she could not see because the water was in her eyes.

How often we find ourselves in a similar position: excited by the prospect of God's promises to us, that is, until the promise comes closer and does not look anything like what we thought it would. If the truth be known, God's promise in reality will more than likely bear no resemblance to the picture we have pictured in our minds. So, when our imagined version meets the reality of God's promise, we find ourselves, perhaps, in many ways like my daughter, standing on the edge of this vast pool of promise, screaming instead of rejoicing, panicking instead of stepping out, faithless instead of faithful, retreating instead of embracing, in fear instead of encouraged, hiding away when we really should be diving in!

The Bible tells us about Saul, the first man to be anointed king of Israel and how he could not be found on the day of his inauguration. He was hiding among the baggage when he was finally found. (See 1 Samuel 10:22.)

Sometimes, in reality, the vastness of God's promise will cause you to want to run and hide. Moses told God that he could not carry out the task to which God was calling him. He made one excuse after another, just to avoid going down to Egypt. But God would have none of it. I once heard someone say that if you can completely comprehend the vision of God, it is not from God. Why? Because when God makes you a promise, or gives you a vision, it will always be bigger than you can imagine, understand, or make sense of. But listen, God has never made a mistake and He never will! If He has picked you for a job, then you are more than equipped to carry it out!

Now I do not know what sort of picture my daughter had in her mind of what the swimming baths would be like, but there is one thing of which I am sure—the reality certainly did not fit the bill, and neither will our picture match God's! Yet, still, amidst all our screams for help when reality hits home, if we stop to listen for just one moment, we will hear God in some way calmly telling us, "It's not as deep, dangerous, scary, or impossible as you think, my child; just put your feet down. You can stand in this, trust me."

Ambiguity comes from a refusal to trust God, so you must trust God. No matter how big the promise, or no matter how impossible it looks, you will not drown and you *can* stand. You will never know you can do it until you try. So stop running, stop hiding, stop screaming, stop convincing yourself why you cannot and begin slowly but surely to put the feet of your faith down into God's promise.

Gloss-Coated Cross

We have all attended conferences from time to time and that is good; I encourage our attendance of them. But when the conference is over and we are hoarse from repeating the name of Jesus; when the lights are switched off; and the doors are closed; when everyone has gone home, we must be sure that our walk with God is in no way based on hype, excitement, or artificial fabrication. We must be sure that our walk is a real one.

Grievous enticing wolves are by cunning persuasion, secretly attempting to change the perception of the people of God from the old rugged cross to a glossy superficial one. It is a glossy cross that omits the need for self-denial, obedience, and suffering. The attempts of these wolves are sugarcoating the cross for their own gain.

But Jesus said, "If any man will come after me, let him deny himself, and take up his cross, and follow me" (Matt. 16:24). The cross marks suffering, no matter how some seek to coat it. It marks, however, suffering for a worthy cause—a life of walking in Christ.

If we read Hebrews 11, God's hall of faith, we will see that it does not portray any glamorous glossy images of walking with God. As a matter of fact, it is enough to make you want to drop your cross and run. For though it very much speaks of faith and how many before overcame through faith, it also shows us, in verses 36 and 37, that sometimes the pathway of faith can become incredibly rough. And though this scripture serves as a source of great inspiration for many, it seeks not to encourage us through blinkers, or to shield us from the reality of how our faith sometimes will be brutally tried and taken to the limits.

The glory of heaven's cross leads to eternal life, that is certain, but the glory of this gloss-coated cross offers everything, but delivers nothing at all; it is all an elaborate illusion. Like the fig tree, it is professing without possessing. (See Mark 11:13.) We must be careful that we do not buy the gloss and become like the fig tree, all show and no essence, no reality, caught up in hype, wearing an artificial glory, gleaned without suffering, empty fruitless individuals, void of true relationship with God, and void of power and authority. The Bible calls it a form of godliness. (See 2 Timothy 3: 5.)

We have to be sure that we are following God for the right reasons. When Jesus was traveling with His disciples, a scribe approached Him, asking whether he could follow Him. Jesus said to the man, "The foxes have holes, and the birds of the air have nests; but the Son of man hath not where to lay his head" (Matt. 8: 20).

Jesus read the man's heart. He knew that he wanted to follow Him for all the wrong reasons. If you think about it, Jesus' reputation must have gone before Him. I can imagine that there were those who thought that Jesus lived a life of relative ease and luxury—one which was in the top band of society and wealth.

161

Perhaps this man was looking for notoriety and afflu-ence, but Jesus soon corrected him, by showing him that His life was not a path of glamour, nor palace courtyards. Note, we do not read where this man challenges Jesus' statement. Surely if he genuinely wanted to follow Jesus, he would have given some form of objection. But on closer examination, we find that his agenda was not in line with Jesus'.

There is, to my mind, a note of caution for all who would seek to follow Christ in the twenty-first century; and that is, we must be sure that we are truly following Him, not personalities, not notoriety, not popularity or wealth. Of course there is only one true cross, however. Satan's endeavour is to have us accept a gloss-covered one, specifically designed to ensnare us. So be careful that you have indeed picked up the cross of which Jesus spoke when He said, "If any man will come after me, let him deny him-self, and take up his cross, and follow me" (Matt. 16:24).

Glory Bearers

From the banks of the Red Sea, the glory of God still shines fervently through the ages. There, it only took one man who was willing to undress himself of pride (with God's help of course), to stand humbly, clothed in the power of the Creator, to move the mighty waters. Moses planted his faith in the fertile soil of divinity; He submit-ted his whole self, a vessel unto God. So transparent was he that the glory of God found an unhindered and unin-hibited place in him and shone brightly.

The waters of the Red Sea recognized the glory that radi-ated from Moses. The waves stood to attention, saluting the presence of the Creator in Him, recognizing that the God of all creation was about to pass through their midst.

As Moses was, so are we receptacles of God's glory. The light of such knowledge deserves our awe—that God should choose to take up residence in us! To think—that we are carriers of His glory! With this honor and responsibility, how then can we expect our lives to be ordinary or run-of-the-mill?

The Bible declares, "The angel of the LORD encampeth round about them that fear him" (Ps. 34:7). We are tabernacles that show God's glory! We are Bethel, the house of God, and wherever we are, the glory of God will shine forth! It is true to say that you are His glory carrier. One of our great challenges, as sons of God, is to remain focused, to remember that regardless of how miraculous the wonders, or how much "greater works" we accomplish, we are not *the* source, but merely the conduits of God's power.

The spirit of pride, which so subtly ensnared many a great man and woman will continue to do so if we fail to remain humble at the feet of the Master. As splendid as Buckingham Palace is, the tourists will affirm that their main focus is not so much the palace as it is the royals, particularly the queen.

Even one glimpse of her would make standing all day in the cold wet weather worth it. It is her presence that changes the palace from mere bricks and mortar to a magnetic attraction. She is the glory of that place; after all, what is a palace without a king or a queen? And by the same token, who are we, in all our splendor, without God's inhabiting presence?

When Diana, Princess of Wales, died, the world, especially England, was plunged into mourning. Thousands of people began to gather outside the palace, not to see the palace, but to see the queen; to know that she was in residence; to somehow be close to her; to share in her grief. But they were informed that she was not actually there, but at her home in Balmoral, Scotland.

A public outcry went up. They wanted the queen in the palace! It was not enough to simply have the palace standing there, despite its beauty! People wanted and, dare I say, needed more! They needed the queen, not the palace. Without the queen Buckingham Palace was merely an empty monument.

We must never fool ourselves into believing that what we achieve is by our own strength—that it is about us! It is not about us—it is about God! Just as in an earlier chapter, I encouraged you not to allow your burdens to bury you, so I implore you not to allow the heights God allows you climb to dizzy your thinking and cloud your vision.

No matter how high the Lord would lift us, we must always remember that it is God and God alone who allows *His* light to shine through us. Never speak from your head, but rather from your heart, for the heart will speak far sounder things than your head ever will. The apostle Paul reminds us not to think of ourselves more highly than is necessary. (See Romans 12:3.) It is far more edifying and beautiful to listen to one who speaks with the love, wisdom, and heart that comes from God than one who speaks from a head comsumed with highmindedness. By all means allow the glory of God to be seen in your life; surrender your will to His, and keep clean the windows of your soul; for God is looking for those who would take up the challenge of bearing His glory while remaining humble.

Sweetened to Her Taste

You Have to Have a Dream

Our ability to dream is not something we should shy away from or even discourage. I believe it is a gift; the power to dream can be an incredible tool if nurtured wisely. For when one dares to believe in a dream, something magical and wonderful begins to happen.

Each of us has this wonderful ability, the ability to dream! Now do not misunderstand the word *dream*. I am not speaking of some whimsical flight of fancy. I am speaking of a yearning that calls more loudly than a room full of people, one that stirs you in the midnight hour, that catapults you to another time, place, role, and dimension. It is a dream that is so clear, so loud, so bright that it consumes your thoughts and inspires you to believe that it can be, regardless of how impossible it seems.

Isn't it strange that dreaming is so strongly discouraged when we are adults, even though we were encouraged to do so in childhood? I dreamed all the time as a child, so why and how am I supposed to stop now? Some of my childhood dreams have been fulfilled, but others have yet to come to pass. Have I stopped dreaming? No. *Will* I stop dreaming? No! For to stop dreaming is to close the eyes of my very soul and cover the ears of my heart to God's incredible impossibilities, to shut out the light and remain in darkness.

What you have to understand is that you inherit your ability to dream from the Father himself. Yes, God! He indeed was the first dreamer. God dreamed, had a vision in simple terms—of an earth. When God began to make clear His vision, or His dream, the light, trees, sky, moon, and sun formed. Creation appeared. What a dream! What a vision!

You see, the power of a dream transcends human understanding. It is not bound by logic or laws, often appearing to be the opposite of the circumstances we face. Was it logical for God to believe that something wonderful could come from a vast mass of ruin? A dream said yes. How could such beauty—that of the earth—come out of such dark nothingness? The answer is—by a dream, one not merely seen, but spoken forth and then acted upon.

You might say, "Yes, but God is God; He could just make His dream come to pass." Yet the Book of Genesis shows us that God worked at it. Just because you see the dream or the vision does not mean that it is not going to take effort and determination to bring it to fruition. Look at what God did: He dreamed it, He believed it, He spoke it, it happened! Believe the vision, for although it might tarry, it will surely come to pass.

What made a lowly Baptist preacher stand in the middle of a then-hostile faction of America, which was consumed with bigotry and fear, and cry peace in the midst of fighting, trusting for something better? A dream! What made a frail, elderly woman stoop down in the mud and muck of the slums of India and believe that she could make a difference to the lives of starving, dying people? A dream! What made a black man, under constant threat of death, take on the might of a nation steeped in racism and segregated by apartheid and rise from thirty years of imprisonment to become that same nation's president? A dream! Is your dream any less possible than theirs? Not in the eyes or capacity of God! So, my friend, you have to have a dream.

If you are to rise from the ashes of your circumstances, you must first ask God to empower you to visualize yourself above them; for if you see it, you will soon begin to speak it, and if you can speak it, you will very soon begin to act out your words, and words acted upon are dreams come true.

Listen, God had the greatest dream of all time, a vision so clear that it compelled Him to send His Son to accomplish it—a dream of mankind, free from the power of sin, death, and hell. So strong was this dream of our Father that it cost Him His Son, and it cost His Son His life. How clear is *your* dream? How strong?

Know this: the cost of an accomplished dream has proved to be high; yet, history has shown us countless numbers of men and women who have been willing to pay its price in blood, pain, sweat, and tears.

The Bible tells of a boy called Joseph who had a dream and dared to utter it. It is one thing to have a dream, but do you have the conviction to believe it and to suffer the reactions, tests, and responsibility of your dream?

When Joseph told his dream, it roused the murderous, jealous hatred of his brothers. They stripped him of his coat and threw him into a pit, leaving Joseph for dead. Love me, hate me, beat me, curse me—but you cannot kill my dream! Deep down in the bottom of the pit Joseph lay, with no coat, no family, no friends—just his dream and a God who would bring it to pass! Satan hates dreamers, visionaries, pioneers, and trailblazers and will do everything in his power to get them to abandon their dreams.

Where many fall foul of him is that they fail to realize that although the dream is spoken in the here-and-now, it is not often intended for the here-and-now, but for later! It will often speak of and reveal things that no one, except the recipient, can hear or see. So, if you are one of God's dreamers (and He has many), do not expect anyone else to see it if God has not specifically shown it to them. Expect to be scorned for your dream, lied about for it, even run out of town because of it. Nevertheless, hold on to it! Do not let it go; for, as I live and as my soul lives, if it was given to you by God, then it *shall* come to pass!

There will be times when the dream you carry seems quite impossible to accomplish, when giving up will appear to be the best option. There will be times, when you will look for someone, anyone, to stand with you, but you will find no one—yet, do not let go of your dream! Hold onto it! Believe it! Trust it! For He who gave it to you is more than able to accomplish it in you!

What more can I say to you than what I already have? Push! Push with everything you are, with everything you hope or dream! Push with all the strength you possess!

Push through the pains that raise their heads, don't waste your pain, for only then will you bear witness to and behold God's unfolding wonder, the manifestation of His glory, His miracle—you!

Chenfor Exxx